Richard Gordon was born in 1921. He qualified as a doctor and then went on to work as an anaesthetist at St Bartholomew's Hospital, and then as a ship's surgeon. As obituary-writer for the *British Medical Journal*, he was inspired to take up writing full-time and he left medical practice in 1952 to embark on his 'Doctor' series. This proved incredibly successful and was subsequently adapted into a long-running television series.

Richard Gordon has produced numerous novels and writings, all characterised by his comic tone and remarkable powers of observation. His *Great Medical Mysteries* and *Great Medical Discoveries* concern the stranger aspects of the medical profession whilst his *The Private Life of…* series takes a deeper look at individual figures within their specific medical and historical setting. Although an incredibly versatile writer, he will, however, probably always be best-known for his creation of the hilarious 'Doctor' series.

BY THE SAME AUTHOR
ALL PUBLISHED BY HOUSE OF STRATUS

Great Medical Mysteries

Richard Gordon

HOUSE OF
STRATUS

This edition published in 2001 by House of Stratus, an imprint of
Stratus Books Ltd., 21 Beeching Park, Kelly Bray,
Cornwall, PL17 8QS, UK

www.houseofstratus.com

Typeset, printed and bound by House of Stratus.

A catalogue record for this book is available from the British Library
and the Library of Congress.

ISBN 1-84232-518-3
EAN 978-184232-518-6

Things are seldom what they seem,
Skim milk masquerades as cream;
Highlows pass as patent leathers;
Jackdaws strut in peacock's feathers.

Black sheep dwell in every fold;
All that glitters is not gold;
Storks turn out to be but logs;
Bulls are but inflated frogs.

Little Buttercup
in *HMS Pinafore*

Contents

CONTENTS

Ah! Sweet Mystery of Life

'A bawd, sir? fie upon him! he will discredit our mystery,' the executioner objects to his new assistant in *Measure for Measure* by William Shakespeare or Francis Bacon or Christopher Marlowe.

Science too has mysteries as solemn as hanging or authorship.

Did the universe start with a big bang or a black hole? Where have all the dinosaurs gone? Does your draining bathwater change direction as your cruise liner crosses the equator?

Medicine lies in science's penetralia, its mysteries intriguingly intimate.

Why do men who shake the world relish the most peculiar treatment from the oddest doctors? Why are razor-minded philosophers hopelessly muddle-headed about their bodies? Is eating people really wrong? Why do women give birth not always to children? Why are we obsessed by Freudian psychology but have the vaguest idea what it is? Why are doctors such messy murderers? What is really happening at Lourdes? And in Loch Ness?

Sadly, medicine has more menacing mysteries in the causes of diseases which kill, disable or make us mad.

Luckily, its determined practitioners will one day solve many of them.

Occasionally bawdily, but I hope never discreditingly, I unfold the more spectacular mysteries of my profession.

PART ONE

The Great Medical Mysteries of History

1 Why Did Mary Toft Give Birth to Seventeen Rabbits?

On Saturday 23 April 1726, illiterate, slow-witted, surly, lazy, five-weeks-pregnant Mary Toft, weeding a field at the village of Godlyman in the county of Surrey, was startled by a jumping rabbit. While a fellow weeder fruitlessly tried trapping it, another rabbit leapt at Mary from the hedge. She was scared. Everyone knew that meeting a hare or rabbit gave the baby a deformed lip, unless you instantly stooped and tore your petticoat.

Mary already had three children, at nineteen had married Joshua Toft, a tailor's drudge. She was dumpy, big-breasted, large-mouthed, placid-faced, cow-eyed, fair-haired with thick straight eyebrows, twenty-five, born in the village. Godlyman is now the London outpost of Godalming, thicker with stockbrokers than with rabbits.

That night she dreamed of rabbits. She was sitting in a field stroking a brace in her lap. She woke with morning sickness, followed by an overwhelming desire to eat rabbit.

Pica (Latin for the promiscuously pecking magpie) is a craving for unnatural food. It is a long-recognized disease, which appeared in Thomas Gale's *Antidotarie Conteyning Hidde and Secret Medicines* of 1563. A nasty case in 1584 ate nothing but pitch. Six-month-old babies eat anything within reach – cigarettes, soap, diamond earrings, their own excreta. Women in early pregnancy send husbands scouring for strawberries in January, oysters in July, bananas, quails, profiteroles, tripe any time. Nobody knows why. But newly pregnant women are believed to enjoy taste and smell of such delicate hypersensitivity that they could write about wine for the Sunday papers.

3

Joshua Toll suffered the humiliation of a man too poor to satisfy a wife's fancies. A labourer's diet was bread and cheese, small beer (1^1/2d a day), potatoes and a 4/- joint on Sundays. A rabbit cost 1/6. You could get three pounds of sugar for that.

In mid-August Mary was six months pregnant. She suffered two attacks of colic with vaginal bleeding and the extrusion of a small fleshy lump. The pregnancy continued. September came, season for hop-picking, inconvenienced for her by a profuse flow of milk from her breasts. On Tuesday 27 September she was clutched with violent pains at night and sent for her mother-in-law, who was a midwife and delivered her of the lungs and intestines of a pig.

Joshua was mystified. He put the entrails in a sack, walked five miles to the county town of Guildford, and displayed them to the locally respected surgeon and man-midwife, Mr John Howard, who rode to Godlyman and delivered Mary of more pig. Nobody reached any conclusion, except that God moved in a mysterious way. A fortnight later Mary was churched, thanking Him for delivery 'from the great pain and peril of Child-birth' like the most respectable and fruitful woman in the village.

In October, Mr Howard was back. Mary was in labour, producing five rabbits. It was a dramatic confinement. The poor animals were leaping inside her for hours, the violent snapping of their bones was audible through the bedclothes, all were stillborn. She continued having rabbits, one a day. Mr Howard was so busy with the case that his other patients were neglected. He moved her into lodgings at Guildford, where she carried on rabbiting. On Wednesday 9 November Mr Howard released, 'twelve rabbits in all had been born to Mary Toft and more were expected.'

The press is ever obsessed with obstetrics. In the summer of 1936, the Dionne quins bawled Hitler's Night of the Long Knives off the front pages. Next year, Britain's St Neots' quads upstaged a new Duke of Kent. Today, a multiple royal test-tube birth would leave no room in the London papers for the racing and cricket.

On the Friday before Palm Sunday 1276, the Countess of Henneberg entered Dutch history with 365 babies 'in bigness all like newbred mice', half sons, half daughters, the odd one an hermaphrodite. The Bishop of

Utrecht had a christening problem. He took the soft option, employing a pair of fonts to call all the males John and all the girls Elizabeth (no record of episcopal ingenuity with the hermaphrodite). The Countess had brought the obstetrical catastrophe on herself by haughtily denying alms to a widow with twins, and after the ceremony rightly dropped dead with all her children. The story in the chronicles must be true, the double font in Loosduinen church outside The Hague is still there to prove it.

Mary Toft's story broke in the *Whitehall Post* of 26 November. News of a wondrous maternal warren buzzed round London. The 43-year-old Prince of Wales was fascinated. The Hanoverians had sat on the English throne a dozen years. George I – with 'blowsy foreign women for his mistresses' – could communicate with Prime Minister Robert Walpole only in their common language of appalling Latin. Son George (also into mistresses) at once dispatched to Guildford his Secretary, the Hon. Mr Molyneux, amateur astronomer and telescope-maker, with the Royal Surgeon, Mr St André, a successful Swiss, surgeon to the Westminster Hospital Dispensary, linguist, fencing-master, dancing-master, lacking only medical qualifications.

They arrived at Guildford by coach-and-four at 2.30 on the afternoon of Tuesday 15 November, the fifteenth rabbit expected any minute. (Had Mary been a real bunny, her pregnancy would have lasted twenty-eight days, she would have produced six litters of five to seven rabbits every year, and become a grandmother every six months.) She was in bed in her stays, amid an adulatory court of local women. Within minutes, she had half a rabbit. It was skinned, the chest containing the heart, which was malformed, and the lungs, which Mr St André found to float in a jar of water.

The patient was cheerful. Mr St André examined her vaginally, discovering bumps in her right Fallopian tube, in which he assumed the rabbits gestated. One breast had a sparse trickle of milk. Pulse normal. Tongue red. Urine specimen unobtainable. Two hours later she suffered pains so violent that five women could barely restrain her, to be delivered of the other half; which fitted exactly into the first. It was a boy.

The guts contained pellets of rabbit dung and spicules of bone. Mr St André found her vagina empty, the uterine cervix – which during pregnancy sticks into the vault of the vagina like the knotted neck of an inflated balloon – was tightly closed. Ten minutes later Mary had a rabbit skin, rolled in a ball. Then the head, with fur but one-eared. The doctor prescribed a sedative and left.

Mr St André returned to London with rabbits Numbers 1, 3, 5, and 9 preserved in spirits of wine. The first was a peculiar rabbit. It had a cat's paws and a cat's chest, its lungs and heart in its neck. The other bodies were jointed as for rabbit stew, but the bits fitted together to make the best part of four rabbits. The heart and bones were immature, the teeth and claws unblunted by use. They would have been – reconstructed – wholly unremarkable babies if born to another rabbit.

At Windsor Castle they were talking of little else. On Sunday 20 November, Herr Cyriacus Ahlers, Surgeon to His Majesty's Hanoverian Household, went to see for himself. Mr Howard locked the bedroom door behind them, excluding the Royal Surgeon's travelling companions – a crowd might upset the patient. The nurse – the patient's sister – announced solemnly that Mary had just had a rabbit skin. Herr Ahlers asked embarrassingly how a rabbit became skinned *en route*. Oh, pressure of the womb against the pubic bones, Mr Howard told him.

Mary was shuffling in her stays across the floorboards, thighs tight together, another rabbit surely crouched to pop out. Mr Howard and Herr Ahlers had hit it off, and were exchanging funny stories. Mary started shouting, screaming. twisting, but they had reached the punch line and she joined the laugher. She's as strong as a horse, Mr Howard explained airily. He examined her in a fireside chair, the ill-burning charcoal in the grate shrouding patient and doctor in smoke.

Mr Howard offered Herr Ahlers a turn. Sticking out of the vagina he found the back half of a skinned rabbit, which he safely delivered with Mr Howard backseat driving (as he knew no midwifery). When he started feeling inside for the rest of the rabbit the jokey mood evaporated, and red-faced Mr Howard forbade further interference with his patient. Furthermore, said Mr Howard, after his own great trouble – not to mention Mary's – might Herr Ahlers see his way to proposing His Majesty granted them both a pension?

Mary started screaming again, and produced the rabbit's front end. Mr Howard suggested dinner. But what about the baby's head? Herr Ahlers asked in alarm. He confessed himself gravely concerned with the patient's condition. Joviality returned. Mr Howard, nurse and Mary roared with laughter at such finicky notions. Herr Ahlers gave her a guinea.

Over the pudding, the Royal Surgeon was struck with an attack of giddiness, sore throat and headache. At five o'clock he left abruptly for an eight-hour journey with coach lamps struggling against the night. He brought his rabbit with him. He found that the lungs floated, there was hay and corn in the gut, and the body seemed divided by a knife. But he left everyone in Guildford delighted. He had seemed convinced that the rabbits were fair game. Mary swore before the Mayor 'that Mr Ahlers declared it was wonderful that people would not believe a fact, that was so true as this appeared to him'. She signed it with her mark, a double cross.

On Wednesday 23 November, Mr St André, the Swiss, was back after more rabbits. Mr Howard regretted that the burrow seemed empty. Poor Mary was now ill with severe right-sided abdominal pain, vaginal bleeding, irregular pulse, blood and pus in the urine. That evening she extruded from her vagina a roll of membrane six inches wide. Next day the surgeon returned to London, but on Sunday a messenger was riding hard with express information from Mr Howard that the rabbits were leaping again.

The King himself was Mary's latest fan. That Saturday. Mr St André had flourished his dissected rabbits under His Majesty's eyes. George I was convinced, thus the story must be true. He dispatched Mr St André again to Guildford, with Sir Richard Manningham, Doctor of Medicine and Bachelor of Laws at Cambridge University, London's top man-midwife.

The man-midwife was a controversial new-fangled practitioner. England's first was a Huguenot refugee, the surgeon Peter Chamberlen, who took over the miscarriage of Charles I's Queen Henrietta Maria when the midwife 'swooned with fear' at the royal bedside. He invented the obstetrical forceps, so frightening to the patient that the clinking metal was muffled with leather so that they might be applied stealthily. The French had a flair for man-midwifery. Julien Clément attended Louis XIV's mistress Madame de Montespan in 1670, for the second of their seven illegitimate children, so impressing the King that he summoned Clément to deliver his daughter-in-law at Versailles twelve years later.

The Dauphine was sickly, twice already miscarried, the labour long and difficult. The room was crowded with attendants, the noisy corridors jammed with courtiers, the diplomatic corps from Paris had asserted its privilege of admission to the bedside. Among the audience wandered the distraught Dauphin and the King issuing orders about the baby's wet-nurse ('she should be dark, healthy and intelligent, and above all must smell delicious').

It was a stifling August. Horses pawed the cobbled courtyard for impatient messengers to bear through France news increasingly likely to be gloomy. To encourage the mother, the bed with bearing-down handles on which two queens of France had given birth was displayed in the chamber, also the relics of St Margaret. The patient grew so feeble that the King declared himself reconciled to the indignity of her safely producing a girl. Only the man-midwife remained inspiringly unruffled, telling everyone not to worry.

After a labour of thirty hours, the King could proclaim: 'We have got a Duc de Bourgogne.' The Dauphin went hunting. The magical man-midwife administered puerperal therapy, flaying a live sheep at the bedside and wrapping the patient in the bloody fleece. He received the title *Accoucheur* and to medicine was born a new speciality – an immensely lucrative one, it becoming as unthinkably unfashionable to give birth with the assistance of a midwife as to dress with the assistance of a parlour-maid rather than a lady's-maid.

Men-midwives were unpopular with their surgical colleagues for demeaning the profession by trivial meddling, with the midwives for taking the bread out of their mouths ('a great horse godmother', Mrs Nihell the Haymarket midwife referred to an eminent one), and with the mothers for transforming a fundamental domestic activity into an operation like cutting for a stone.

Three hundred years later they are obstetricians, patchily unpopular with women for denying joyous natural childbirth (which unhappily is a retrospective process, joyous only if all goes as well as a hen laying an egg), for selfishly usurping the 'birthing process', and for impairing freedom to have babies in trendy positions advised in the Sunday papers, on all fours, standing up, as Chinese peasants squatting in paddy-fields, or as a branch of aquasports.

Sir Richard Manningham was faultlessly respectable. He was the son of a bishop. He was, like Robert Boyle, Sir Christopher Wren and Samuel Pepys, elected to the Royal Society. He invented 'lying-in' wards. He was keen. On Monday 28 November, he left London with Mr St André at 4.00 a.m. arriving in Guildford at noon.

Mary Toft was in bed. The score was then seventeen. Her courtiers proclaimed gravely that the rabbits had not been leaping since midnight. He decided to administer the hot cloths. Mary started shaking violently, the bed rattled despite several women sitting on it. Sir Richard retired to the White Hart.

Within the hour, Mr Howard hastened with a scrap of newly delivered membrane wrapped in paper. He said it was part of the next rabbit's caul. Sir Richard said it was a slice of pig's bladder. A breathless messenger announced that Mary Toft was in action. Sir Richard hurried from the pub pushing back his cuffs, and found the uterine cervix tight shut, but produced from her vagina tissue which he said was pig's bladder. All the women in the room began to cry at so dreadful an implication. He asked, Well, has anyone got some pig's bladder, then we can see? They had a bit in the house. (*Ha ha!* thought Sir Richard.) He sniffed both and declared they smelled of pig piss.

He had a hot argument over the punch in the White Hart with Mr St André, who maintained that if Mary could give birth to rabbits she could give birth to pigs' bladders. It was the same scientific principle. Then they took the carriage to London, Sir Richard *marking the bladder with a small notch*.

It was time for the show to be brought into the West End. Next day Mary was borne to Leicester Fields near fashionable Covent Garden, and installed in Mr Lacy's Bagnio – an eighteenth-century sauna and massage parlour. Mr Molyneux simultaneously provided a useful quote, 'that he did not perceive the least circumstance of fraud in the conduct of the affair while he was in Guildford'.

'Great numbers of the nobility have been to see her,' said the *London Journal* of 3 December. The coach wheels jammed, the sedan chairs lurched together, gorgeously dressed ladies and gentlemen crammed her bedroom.

It was better than the Dauphine's childbed at Versailles. The Age of Reason was the age of credulity. Berkley and Hume co-existed with the South Sea Bubble, with a hundred companies 'for improving the art of making soap…for the trasmutation of quicksilver into a malleable fine metal…for furnishing funerals to any part of Great Britain…for erecting houses and hospitals for taking in and maintaining illegitimate children, capital two millions…for a wheel for perpetual motion, capital one million…for carrying on an undertaking of great advantage, but nobody to know what it is'.

Sir Richard circulated the notched bladder among his friends the Dukes of Richmond and Montague and Lord Baltimore. They thought it was pig, too. Mary meanwhile had two hours of fits, with 'rolling of the eyes, during which she would make a whining noise'.

On Sunday 4 December, Sir Richard brought to the Bagnio Dr James Douglas, obstetrician to Queen Caroline, collector of several hundred thousand editions of Horace, discoverer of the Pouch of Douglas, which every woman carries behind her womb. Sir Richard decided something was going to happen. Mary was having labour pains, her uterus a big, soft lump above the pubis, clearly fully loaded, the cervix was starting to open like a cat's eye in the dark. Dr Douglas agreed. The time was three in the afternoon. At six that evening, another Mr Howard – Thomas, porter at the Bagnio – resolved the case by confessing to His Majesty's Justice of the Peace that he was smuggling in rabbits.

Mary was arrested in bed. She protested that the rabbits were for her supper. She loved rabbit. Everyone knew that. Sir Richard kept her out of jail, using royal clout. She lay in the Bagnio as a captive of the High Constable of Westminster, while Sir Richard gave her Gestapo treatment. He told Mary she had some anatomical peculiarity enabling her to stick bits of rabbit into her womb. Without the truth, 'he would have to try a very painful experiment on her'. On Wednesday morning she confessed.

In Guildford, Edward Costen and Richard Stedman divulged that they had kept Joshua Toft supplied with rabbits – what he could not afford to eat was acceptable as a business expense. On the Saturday, Herr Ahlers published a pamphlet, *Some Observations Concerning the Woman of Godlyman in Surrey*, revealing he 'had a violent suspicion of the whole matter and feigned a great compassion for the woman's case'. He placed an advertisement in the *Daily Journal*, depicting an honest doctor fallen among frauds, from whom he shammed a sick headache in Guildford to escape. Mr John Howard took sixteen lines in the *Whitehall Evening Post* to recant as indignantly. Sir Richard Manningham rushed out *An Exact Diary of What was Observed During Active Attendance upon Mary Toft from Nov. 28 to Dec. 7, 1726*. Dr James Douglas rushed out a contradiction to everything in it.

Mary was prosecuted as a vile cheat – it was all in next Tuesday's *St James's Evening Post* – under a law of Edward III, who died in 1377. The English have a fondness for rubbing noses in their history. She was locked up in Bridewell Prison, beyond Westminster Abbey in Tothill Fields, crammed with Londoners hoping to bribe a glimpse of her. The fuss was sustained gleefully into 1727. Broadsheet and ballad created Mary as splendid a national hero as all twelve Great Train Robbers 237 years later. Most took her side. A doctor's face always fits the pillory.

The *Doctors in Labour or a New Whim Wham from Guildford* was a popular number with the street singers.

> They're welcome all to Mary – all that will
> May in her Warren for a rabbit feel

trilled from the cobblestones. Sir Richard Manningham's threatened experiment was well known to be sending a chimney-sweep's boy up her Fallopian tubes. Then Alexander Pope applied his subcutaneous quill.

On Tuesday 20 December appeared a four-page anonymous pamphlet, *The Discovery: or, The Squire turn'd Ferret. Ballad to Tune of High Boys! up go we; Chevy Chase; Or what you please*. Pope was the author. He had the clinical details from Mr St André, who was treating him for a painful hand after an accident, and came out of the poem less bloodily flayed than Manningham, Douglas, Molyneux, Howard or His Royal Highness.

It began,

> Most true it is, I dare to say,
> E'er since the Days of Eve,
> The weakest Woman sometimes may
> The wisest man deceive.

At Godlyman, hard by the *Bull*,
A Woman long thought barren,
Bears *Rabbits* – Gad! so plentiful,
You'd take her for a warren.

St André and Molineux arrive,

Resolv'd this Secret to explore,
And search it to the Bottom.

The Surgeon with a Rabbit came,
And first to pieces cut it;
Then slyly thrust it up *that same*,
As far as man could put it.

Astronomer Molyneux suggests,

Now that her legs are ope,
If ought within we may descry
By Help of Telescope.

The instrument himself did make,
He rais'd and level'd right
But all about was so opake,
It could not aid his sight.

Is it alive? St-A-d-ré cry'd;
It is; I feel it stir.
Is it full grown? The Squire reply'd
It is; see here's the FUR.

Douglas had the honour of making the *Dunciad* –

There all the learn'd shall at the labour stand,
And Douglas lend his soft, obstetric hand.

12

'London is divided into factions about it,' Pope noted in early December. The doctors as usual responded to attack by the public by attacking each other. Medical men who had never seen a rabbit emerge from anything more startling than a piecrust fiercely took sides. Hogarth's *Cunicularii* shows Mary Toft groaning in labour amid flapping bed-curtains, surrounded by her readily identifiable doctors, the floor running with rabbits. It was commissioned by some London surgeons at a guinea apiece. They had not witnessed such fun for years. Hogarth was always as eager to cartoon physicians – in huge wigs, sniffing the aromatic, prophylactic herbs in their gold-headed canes – as other destructive evils like gin and prostitution.

I venture the first diagnosis of the Mary Toft mystery in 250-odd years.

When frightened by the rabbit in April, Mary was five months, not five weeks, pregnant. The difference would have been unnoticeable in so diminutive a podgy girl. In mid-August she produced not a fleshy lump but a dead full-term baby, to be secretly buried or burned. Thus her breasts would create milk, flowing normally during the hop-picking of early September, barely a trickle expressible by Mr St André two months afterward.

When Mary suffered pain and vaginal discharge on the night of 27 September, she called her mother-in-law the midwife. Mary confessed to Sir Richard Manningham that a woman accomplice – unnamed, but it was assuredly a family conspiracy with mother-in-law and sister – stuffed her vagina with the head of a rabbit and the claws and body of a cat. It hurt. The bits of pig which Mr John Howard delivered were lodged more comfortably in the vulva.

Mother-in-law urged that Mary was on to a good thing. Play it right, she could live well without working. Old Mrs Toft would supply the rabbits, for a cut of the profits. Mary asked, for how long? Mrs Toft said discouragingly that a doe's litter could reach thirteen.

Once the show was a success, they went over the top. Once he realized he was operating in a gold mine, Mr John Howard became part of the act. On 20 November he conjured half a rabbit into her vagina in a smoke-screen. Mary luckily never fell to puerperal fever. The eighteenth was an unhygienic century, but dirt breeds antibodies as well as germs. The foreign bodies irritated her, causing pains which she consciously augmented. On 23 November, when Mr St André examined Mary, she was really ill from their trauma and infection. The rabbits were ordinary young ones. Had she borne them, their guts would have been empty of food, their uninflated lungs would have sunk in Mr St André's and Herr Ahlers' jars of water.

Mary was freed from Bridewell. She was back in jail fourteen years later at Guildford, for receiving stolen property. She died in 1763, aged 62, secure in history for cunning and ignorance, hoodwinking eager intelligence as easily as Puck discovering what fools these mortals be.

The mystery of the mystery is the gullible surgeons. The fault lay in their learning and their dereliction.

At the beginning of the eighteenth century, medicine had loosed itself from the crook of the church and was impatiently sorting the ill-assimilated discoveries and philosophies of the Renaissance for everyday use. Science was chaotic, awaiting the law of Newton and the order of Linnaeus. Nobody was sure of the distinction between the scientifically sublime and ridiculous.

An honourable doctor's reason can melt in the hot wind of his enthusiasm. Bernard Shaw's votaries of the nuciform sac were perpetuated in the 1900s by Sir Arbuthnot Lane, who removed the colon for all conditions including suicidal tendencies – in the spouse. In the age of antibiotics and atomic fission, cardiac transplantation is often the operation which kills two patients at once. The miracle of Godlyman could never fool today's sophisticated public, which must dupe itself with extrasensory perception, unidentified flying objects, popular sex guides, popular diets, and the popular psychological doctrines which spray the Californian coast as spectacularly and fatuously as the surf.

'The philosophies of one age have become the absurdities of the next, and the foolishness of yesterday has become the wisdom of tomorrow,' said Edwardian physician Sir William Osler. Medical schools should say a prayer once a year for the soul of Mary Toft.

2 Whose Teeth Did George Washington Eat With?

The year after he became President, George Washington terrified an English visitor: 'His mouth was like no other I ever saw; the lips firm and the under jaw seemed to grasp the upper with force, as if the muscles were in full action when he sat still.'

Conversation must have resembled raising a smile from the Sphinx.

Reason for the frosty reception was not the aftermath of war but the President's new false teeth. They worked like a rat-trap in reverse. Two jaws of beeswax-coated lead were separated by coiled steel springs, so powerful that he needed to clamp his muscles of mastication like a toddler refusing spinach. Weariness, inattention or resignation would have had him greet callers like a demonic mask from *Noh* drama.

'The President seemed to bear in his countenance a settled aspect of melancholy,' Senator William Maclay recalled a large, brilliant dinner party. 'No cheering ray of sunshine broke through the cloudy gloom of settled seriousness.'

He was not missing the point of the jokes. His gums were giving him hell.

'A certain anxiety was visible in his countenance, with marks of extreme sensibility,' recollected another Englishman invited for breakfast in 1794. It was a pappy meal, bread and butter and sliced tongue. Washington's most comfortable dinner was pickled tripe, shipped specially from London. He soused his false teeth overnight in port, because they tasted so filthy.

The mouth which could not tell a lie had terrible teeth. They started falling out from the age of twenty-two. He bought sponge toothbrushes by the dozen, wired false teeth into the gaps with pliers, fought the British with raging toothache. By 1776 he had only one tooth in his head, a lower premolar. This lasted him until sixty-four and you can see it in the New York Academy of Medicine.

His dentist Mr Greenwood of New York (four doors down from the theatre, towards St Paul's church) made him sets of teeth at $15 a time. The dentist's advert quoted the President, 'I shall always prefer your services to that of any other in the line of your present profession.'

The patient was nearing departure from his lifelong habit of veracity. Some sets of teeth were so tormentingly ill-fitting that Washington would frenziedly file down the metal arches, on the biblical principle applicable to eyes and hands. Unlike his table-guests, he never removed his teeth to lay beside his plate while eating. He developed indigestion and short temper.

'It shoots beyond the gums and forces the lip out just under the nose,' he complained, returning one set from Philadelphia. George Washington was always sensitive about his looks. As a young man with most of his teeth, he had a jaw as intimidating as Sherlock Holmes'. When Gilbert Stuart painted him in 1796, the rolls of cotton that Washington stuffed into his mouth replaced cadaverous hollows with a sagging plumpness resembling the aged Queen Victoria. It is sad that this depiction should be his most cherished, being on the dollar bill.

From his wartime days, Washington tended to keep his mouth shut. False teeth made him mumble and turned him from public speaking. How tragic that modern dentistry rescued from a similar decision a politician of comparably awful dentition, Adolf Hitler.

The teeth which scared the Englishman in 1790 weighed three ounces, the equivalent of a pocketful of loose change in your mouth. The upper set had been taken from an animal, probably an elk. The lower were extracted from humans. During the birth of the United States of America, who were those edentulous unknown honoured to chew every mouthful for its Messiah?

3 Was the Marquis de Sade Really
a Kindly Man?

The Marquis de Sade suffered cruelly from his mother-in-law.

On Tuesday 17 May 1763 he married Renée-Pélagie de Montreuil at the church of St Roch by the Jardins des Tuilleries. It was three months after the Treaty of Paris had ended the Seven Years' War, in which Pitt won Canada on the banks of the Elbe. On May Day, the marriage had been blessed at Versailles by Louis XV, Queen Marie and the Dauphin. The clap which the bridegroom caught in April from the daughter of the Marquis de Lauris was better.

Sade at twenty-two was slim and handsome, round-faced, soft-chinned, small-nosed and mouthed, his complexion, like many others', finger-printed by smallpox. He was a cavalry captain, fighting Prussians from the age of fifteen, a man who kept a feather in his hat and a sword at his side. He was always ready for a lark with a tart or a servant girl – or lad. He never missed a ball or party. He was mad about actresses. It all infuriated his father. James Boswell was exactly the same age and having exactly the same trouble in Edinburgh.

The Sades had come to France in the twelfth century from Italy (where they were the Sauzas). They owned a small estate near Avignon in Provence, its square-turreted château on a hill at La Coste. Father was an ambassador. Mother's fifth cousin was Cardinal Richelieu's niece. Uncle was an abbé. The infant Marquis was to be christened Louis-Alphonse-Donatien, but the servants customarily given such jobs got muddled in church and he became Donatien-Alphonse-Françoise.

The wedding was arranged on the sound principles of French cupidity. The country supported a variety of nobility. The needy Sades enjoyed *noblesse de race* – beyond the Duc de Richelieu shimmered some distant relative of royal blood. This had cash value. The Montreuils of Normandy were rich. They ran the Paris *Cour des Aides*, a pre-revolutionary welfare organization raising taxes on wine and salt, with a dependable rake-off. They envied the ancient *noblesse d'epée*, who despised the *noblesse de robe* which had bought its titles from Louis XIV, wholesale. The Comtesse de Sade had retreated to a convent, and refused to allow the Comte to sell her diamonds and pay for the wedding.

The bride was twenty, tall, dark-haired, dark-eyed, elegant. Young Sade fancied her seventeen-year-old sister Anne-Prospère, blue-eyed, fair-haired, a lively schoolgirl. Their mother Marie-Madeleine, barely forty and looking less, was dainty, amusing, charming, quick-witted, domineering. She fancied the bridegroom.

Now read on.

The marriage settlement was as complex as a company merger. The young couple were to be lodged for five years with the Montreuils, given spot cash and an income. The old Comte retained the tatters of his impoverished estates. The Marquis was thenceforward the Montreuils' pensioner.

The excitement and enchantment of marriage, honeymoon and homemaking sustain the delicate new relationship for varying periods, in the Marquis' case six weeks. He rented a house behind iron-spiked walls and stout yellow-painted carriage-doors near the Sorbonne in Paris. He told his wife that he was going to look for work in Fontainebleau. On 20 October, the Montreuils heard he was in jail.

Jeanne Testard was a twenty-year-old fanmaker who moonlighted at Madame de Rameau's high-class brothel, where she was offered forty-eight livres for a special job (5000 livres was a comfortable annual income). A carriage brought her across the Seine and through the yellow gates. Upstairs she met a young man in a blue coat with red collar and silver buttons, who locked the door and asked if she was a good Christian. She said she tried.

He took her into a black-draped room with four birches, five whips and three crucifixes. He suggested mutual flagellation. She said no. He masturbated on a crucifix instead. He spent the night reading her poetry. In the morning, he mooted sodomy. She said no. Or she told the police later that she said no. The penalty for sodomy was death, regardless of passivity or sex.

The man made a date for Sunday morning, so they could take Communion, steal the host, and copulate afterwards with it inserted *per vaginum*. He seemed one of those with weird tastes.

The evening would have rested in the secret silt which forms so broad a stratum of the human mind, had not the King a lively interest in brothels. He was on a percentage of the action, through the taxes. His police were always nosing round them. They knew the Marquis as a connoisseur. Jeanne was questioned by Inspector Marais, with whom Sade was to enjoy the barbed intimacy of Moriarty and Sherlock Holmes. The King read the police report and imprisoned the Marquis in the donjon at Vincennes. 'Everything that concerns God and religion is beyond the forgiveness of men appointed to render justice,' his father counselled wisely and too late.

Madame de Montreuil was appalled, humiliated, furious. Her delightful son-in-law held for *debauche outrée!* The dazzle of the marriage had blinded her to the renown of his odd frolics. She wrote agitatedly to his uncle, the abbé. He could do little to help. He was just out of jail himself on the same charge, after a police raid on an Avignon brothel.

Sade wrote to the Lieutenant-General of Police from his cell, with the convincing eloquence which later rang from *oeuvres* penned in similar bleak ateliers. He implored forgiveness for so foolish a lapse into temptation. The Comte came to petition the King, in tears. On 13 November 1763 the Marquis was exiled to Normandy, escorted by Inspector Marais. Renée-Pélagie became pregnant.

Sade fretted away the summer before skipping back to Paris and setting up house *en garçon* in lonely woods to the south at Arceuil. Mademoiselle Colet was an eighteen-year-old actress at the Comédie Italienne, who could earn 700 livres a night (on the bed, not the boards). Sade got her for 500 livres a month, though on a time-share basis. In between, he brought four girls at a time to the isolation of Arceuil from Madame Le Brissault's brothel by the Barrière Blanche, stripped them and flogged them, but gave them dinner afterwards.

It takes two to tango. 'Actually, whipping a few girls (for a consideration agreed upon in advance) is a rather petty feat,' adjudges Simone de Beauvoir. Everyone was doing it. Ballet girls whipped the Comte de Bintheim until he bled, under a regular arrangement. Whips and birches were as commonplace conveniences in brothels as tapers and newspapers in coffee-houses. *Le vice anglais* was swishing merrily in Sir Francis Dashwood's Hell Fire Club, and warming the affections of John Cleland's Fanny Hill and her customers. The Marquis de Sade did not invent sadism. He only gave it a bad name.

Inspector Marais fussed round the brothels, enjoining them to stop Sade's takeaways. Madame de Montreuil heard about Mademoiselle Colet. She tried disrupting the affair subtly by cataloguing the girl's promiscuity. It shortly ended naturally, when the actress did a Mimi and died.

June 1765. *Vive le Marquis et la Marquise!* At last the bride appeared in La Coste, amid villagers waving their hats in respectful enthusiasm. With admirable *noblesse oblige,* Sade lavishly entertained the local gentry. He refurbished the chateau's disused theatre, writing and directing the shows himself. The polish of the Marquise's performances drew her audiences' breath, even if she was shorter and more vulgar than expected. Uncle the abbé was invited for a week, the hospitality marred only by his awareness that the Marquise was not Renée-Pélagie but Mademoiselle de Beauvoisin from the Paris Opéra ballet.

When Madame de Montreuil castigated the abbé for condoning the outrageous impersonation, he protested that the Marquis never *introduced* the lady as his wife, people just took it for granted, and he had been nowhere near the château, anyway. '*He* always has a couple of whores living with him,' grumbled Sade, when he heard of the correspondence.

Madame de Montreuil sheltered the wife from the escapade with secrecy. In the autumn the Marquis returned to Normandy and Renée-Pélagie became pregnant again. Mademoiselle de Beauvoisin was pregnant already. She had her baby, returned to the stage and bedded with the Foreign Minister, the Duc de Choiseul. In August 1767 Sade's son was born, that January his father had died. The Marquis journeyed briefly to La Coste for the villagers to kneel to him, returning to Paris and tall Mademoiselle Dorville from Madame Hecquet's brothel (only 240 livres a month). He was a bad landlord. He never used the title.

The Ancient Mariner could time his grievous misfortunes from shooting the albatross. Sade as precisely from strolling in the place des Victoires at nine on Easter Sunday morning, 3 April 1768.

In grey coat with white muff and gold-topped cane, he encountered a beggarwoman, thirty-year-old German pastrycook's widow Rose Keller. He suggested three livres for doing the housework. They took a carriage to Arceuil. They went upstairs. The shutters were closed. He lit a candle and told her to undress. She said she was not that sort of a girl. He said, oh, come on, let's have fun, and if you don't I'll kill you and bury you in the garden.

She stripped to her shift. He ripped it off. He threw her face down on the bed. He lashed her hands to one end, feet to the other. He took off his coat and birched her. She screamed. He ordered her to be quiet, or he'd kill her. He nicked her here and there with a small knife, sealing the wounds with wax (he often complained that his ejaculation needed considerable stimulus). He brought boiled beef and brandy and locked her in. She made a rope of blankets and escaped. That evening, the gendarmes called.

Sade was angry. The woman knew perfectly well she was in for an orgy, not to do the floors. Why, two other girls were already there for a *partie de libertinage*. Anyway, he never used a birch, only a cat-o'-nine-tails.

Madame de Montreuil responded as a practical French-woman. She must buy the girl off. The abbé was the go-between. Rose stuck out for 3000 livres, but settled for 2400 and medical expenses. 'At the cost of a rather disagreeable hour or two,' writes her biographer, 'and a few moments of actual discomfort not far removed in degree from a visit to an eighteenth-century dentist, Rose Keller became possessed of more money than she could ever have seen in her life before.' Everyone was happy but the King. Whacking girls on Easter Day was sacrilege. He put Sade inside again.

The story ran round Europe. Madame du Deffand hastened to write all about it to Horace Walpole. The Chambre de Tournelle, the highest criminal court in the land, was to try the culprit (in his absence). Rose Keller was a small nut for the judicial sledgehammer, but the *noblesse dorée* was rumoured to enjoy itself too peculiarly.

The Bourbon Prince de Conti hired flocks of lovely ballet girls, wastefully buggering them. Monsieur Peixotte the banker made naked girls crawl about with peacock feathers inserted *per rectum*. Among the *noblesse de cour*, who Nancy Mitford mentions 'were cooped up in a perpetual house party at Versailles', Madame du Barry cared to watch girls whipped, the Duchesse de la Vallière and the Duchesse de Luxembourg were les, the Princesse d'Enrichemont had her footmen rape the maids. The King's brother the Comte de Charolais invited Madame de Saint-Sulpice to dinner, got her drunk, inserted a firework into her vagina, lit the blue paper and retired. She was in bed for weeks.

And the King! Everyone knew about the Parc-aux-Cerfs at Versailles. Madame de Pompadour perforce tolerated these rivals, even fifteen-year-old cobbler's daughter Louise O'Murphy, delicious all over, as Boucher let us see for ourselves. The *ancien régime* was not sufficiently enfeebled for stone-deafness to public opinion. A scapegoat was needed to show that the worthy authorities disapproved. The notion is enduring. It killed Stephen Ward in 1963.

Sade was escorted to the fortress at Lyons by Inspector Marais. Renée-Pélagie was allowed a visit, and became pregnant. The King relented and signed letters of annulment. These stated majestically that the crime had never happened. Sade was released into exile at La Coste.

Madame de Montreuil insisted that her daughter stay at home rather than risk imprisonment in a remote château with an obvious lunatic. Three years later the Marquis was in jail again, but only for debt. At last he brought his wife Renée-Pélagie to her estate. Also his sister-in-law, Anne-Prospère, who wanted to be a nun. He wrote indecent parts for both of them in his private theatricals. Madame de Montreuil was angered, but the sisters rather liked it.

On the morning of Saturday 17 June 1772, the Marquis took four girls to a house near the port at Marseilles, with his valet dressed as a sailor. He whipped the girls with an iron-studded cat-o'-nine-tails, had them beat him, copulated with them, had his valet copulate with them, masturbated his valet while whipping the girls and sodomized the girls while his valet sodomized him ('Lucky Alphonse, always in the middle'). In fact and fiction, Sade had an ingenious mind for sexual combinations. At the beginning of his novel *Juliette*, a nun and two schoolgirls with a dildo perform $3^5 = 243$ varieties. What would Sade have achieved, had he access to a computer?

The Marquis cut each stroke on the mantelpiece, like a cricketer in an English meadow notching the score, 240 at close of play. He distributed six livres apiece and invited the girls to come boating. To get his money's worth he had also distributed aniseed bon-bons spiked with Spanish fly.

This beetle *Lytta vesicatoria* embodies an oil as irritant to human skin as mustard gas. Or to the stomach, if swallowed. Or to the urinary tract, when excreted. The warmth of this genital inflammation founded its reputation as an aphrodisiac among the characters of Ben Johnson and Beaumont and Fletcher. An overdose brings bloody vomiting and death. A London businessman killed a sexually unsusceptible secretary with it 200 years later.

Afeared she was dying, one of the girls sent for a doctor, who went to the police. The royal prosecutor questioned the quartet and dispatched a mounted posse to La Coste. The Marquis got wind, hurried his wife Renée-Pélagie to buy off the girls in Marseilles and bolted across the Savoy frontier into the authority of the King of Sardinia. He travelled as the Comte de Mazan, his sister-in-law Anne-Prospère as his Comtesse.

Everyone remembered Rose Keller. The story exploded into a fashionable ball where poisoned women ripped off their clothes and roamed Marseilles in nymphomaniacal frenzy. On 3 September, Sade and his valet were sentenced to death in their absence, nobleman on the block, lackey on the gallows. Beforehand, they would kneel bareheaded and barefoot in rough shirts and halters, bearing huge candles and begging forgiveness on the steps of St Marie-Majeure's cathedral. Afterwards, they would be burned and scattered to the winds.

The sentence was executed nine days later at Aix-en-Provence, also in their absence. The authorities thought it reasonable to behead the Marquis more comfortably in effigy, because so few had died for sodomy, and aphrodisiac goodies were so commonplace in society that they were called *pastilles de Richelieu*.

The King's *lettre de cachet* stayed in force. Sade could still be locked up for life. Extradition was an unknown criminal inconvenience, but Madame de Montreuil had her friend the Duc d'Aiguillon, then the French Foreign Minister, get the Sardinian king to oblige by imprisoning the Marquis. After three months he escaped from the Alpine fortress at Chambéry, wandered in Spain, returned warily to La Coste in the autumn.

Soon he was at it again. He established a harem of Renée-Pélagie, her lady-in-waiting, a housemaid, five fifteen-year-old girls and a boy. The housemaid had a baby. The girls escaped. A father shot at Sade, but missed. Early in 1777, the Marquis heard that his mother was dying and risked travelling to Paris with his wife.

His mother was already dead and buried, but Madame de Montreuil had vindictively kept it from him. Provence was harmlessly remote. Paris was dangerous. He was arrested at the Hotel Denmark by Inspector Marais under another *lettre de cachet*. These were delightfully effective instruments for neutralizing tediously wayward members of a family. Once signed by the King and a minister and waxed with the royal seal, the recipient went to prison without the necessity of a trial or even of concocting a reason. He stayed there as long as someone at home was prepared to pay his board and lodging. The Marquis was returned to Vincennes. He was thirty-six, and remained in prison until he was fifty.

Madame de Montreuil kept him there. She had somehow to glue the shattered family reputation. He was making it dreadfully difficult to marry off her remaining daughters. The Marquis wrote for mercy, using his blood as ink. She suggested admitting he was mad, then everyone could overlook the girls in Marseilles. *Tout expliquer c'est tout pardonner.* He refused to part with his sanity. His misery was sharpened by piles, thickening cataracts, a cough and blood-spitting. He had nothing to divert him except writing.

His first was a jolly work, *Dialogue entre un prêtre et un moribond*. The dying man objects to repenting his sins. If God had meant us to resist temptation, he should have created us stronger. It is surely holy to make others as happy as ourselves? He has half-a-dozen lovely naked women next door to enliven his deathbed, but is willing to go shares. The priest is instantly converted to his philosophy.

The Marquis started *Les 120 journées de Sodome* on 22 October 1785 and finished it in thirty-seven days, a forty-foot long, six-inch wide secret roll of paper covered with tiny writing, enough for a 500-page modern book. A duke, a bishop, a politician, a banker and their young wives retire to a château isolated in the Black Forest with eight old women, eight little girls and eight little boys. Also four lusty young male *fouteurs*, who help the four principals physically, much as a Highland gillie obliges a salmon fisherman.

The duke's penis is twelve inches long and eight in circumference, the size of a rolled-up folded copy of *The Times* (the average American male, according to Kinsey, has a penile length of 6.3 inches in erection). He ejaculates not as a sniper but as a machine-gunner. He can drink eighteen bottles of wine before feeling tipsy (three of them while sodomizing the banker).

The duke's fortune is limitless, the comfort faultless, the atmosphere unflaggingly *gemütlich*, the cuisine *trois étoiles* — shellfish soup, twenty-dish *hors d'oeuvre*, chicken breasts, game, roasts, pies, twenty-six sorts of pudding, sugared pastries, ices, chocolates (all served by naked little girls), with burgundy, claret, Tokay, Madeira, six sorts of liqueur and three sorts of coffee. It was worth attending the 120 days of Sodom for the food.

The daily orgies were posted with the brisk, precise authority of the army orders.

If humans did this sort of thing in the street they would assuredly frighten the horses. But Sade's prose has less connection with sexual reality than Daisy Ashford's. His roistering style of anatomical and physiological impossibility has the mocking innocuousness of medical student songs like *The Ball of Kerriemuir*. The more outraged the eavesdroppers, the more the fun. Sadism is the vivid, elaborate, complex fantasy of an energetic writer locked up with nothing for company but his potty.

On 29 February 1784, Sade was transferred from Vincennes to the Bastille. On 14 July 1789, being Bastile Day, the mob stormed it. Sade's cell had a long-spouted tin funnel for urination through the window. He reversed it for a megaphone to urge hasty deliverance by the citizens before his jailers cut his throat. Such quick-witted ingenuity deserves the historical remembrance of Sir Walter Raleigh and his cloak. The Marquis became Citizen Sade. He became legally separated from Renée-Pélagie. His novel *Justine* was published, his play *Le Comte Oxtiern* performed at the *Théâtre Molière*. He set up house with a thirty-year-old actress, Marie-Constance Renelle. Few inhabitants of France benefited better from the Revolution.

The Committee of Public Safety was established on 6 April 1793. *Président* of its subsidiary court which tried counterfeiters was Citizen Sade. 'I am a judge!' he exclaimed. 'Yes, a judge! Assessor for the prosecution!' An early caller was a former *Président* of the *Cour des Aides*, Monsieur de Montreuil. It was their first encounter in fifteen years, which Madame de Montreuil had ensured Sade spent mostly in prison. His father-in-law made himself highly agreeable.

Now Sade could do it for real. He held untramelled power of life and death. It needed but a denunciation. But he was an abolitionist, living in difficult times. He was baffled at the pointlessness of any sentence unaimed at reforming the criminal. Nothing was further from his thoughts than cutting off heads, even his sadistic mother-in-law's. Such unpatriotic and unfashionable squeamishness risked his own.

Compared with Robespierre, Marat and their savage confrères, who had never so much as spanked a girl's bum in their lives and decapitated 2632 Parisians during the 502 days of The Terror, Sade was a merciful and philosophical Christian gentleman. The mob were more casual with cruelty. They decapitated with a sword the Queen's (perhaps too intimate) friend the Princesse de Lamballe, joggled her head on a pikestaff under the Queen's window, dragged her through the streets, sliced off her breasts and her vulva, and fell about when the executioner used her pubic hair for a moustache. The blood on the cobbles reflected Sade's saintliness.

That summer, someone enlightened Marat about Sade's record. On 2 June, Marat denounced him. Through a bureaucratic oversight, liable in the most enthusiastic administrations, the Marquis de Salle was arrested instead, and in obeyance of routine protestingly guillotined. Marat discovered his error on 13 July, but with immense good fortune that evening Charlotte Corday murdered him in his bath.

Sade busied himself with good works among the sick. He became a Hospital Commissioner. His eighty-eight page report on the squalid wards abolished bed-sharing between two or three patients, one perhaps already dead. His cough worsened, he spat more blood, in September he resigned. He first ensured the Montreuils' security on the official list of pre-revolutionary families now beyond risk of suspicion, denouncement and death. 'Such is the revenge I take upon them,' he murmured.

What a nice man!

In December he was arrested again, held for a year in a commandeered convent with a guillotine under his window, its delightful garden a cemetery for its victims. Then he enjoyed his longest liberty since the night with Jeanne Testard, until Napoleon arrested him in 1801. He was transferred to the Charenton lunatic asylum, a morose, aloof, silent man shuffling in a dressing gown and smoking heavily. He died at seventy-six, six months before the Battle of Waterloo. The previous year he had copulated repeatedly with a fifteen-year-old laundress, for a few livres.

'The normal act of sexuality has an aggressive content in that the male inserts his penis into the female, whilst the acceptance of the penis is a submissive act' – so the psychiatrists put it. Masochism goes with sadism as deliciously as ham and eggs. Leopold von Sacher-Masoch was expectedly a softy compared with Sade. A Spanish–Slav–Bohemian born in Poland in 1835, he was already a prosperous and respected novelist and became deeply offended when Krafft-Ebing named a perversion after him in *Psychopathia Sexualis*. Though he *did* have this thing about dressing up as the maid, kissing girls' boots, being bound for a lady wearing her sables to whip him. *Venus in Furs* is as autobiographical as *Mr Norris Changes Trains*.

It has incidents like –

'Wanda!' I run to put my arms round her and kiss her, but she retreats a step and eyes me from head to foot.

'Slave!'

'Mistress!' I kneel and kiss the hem of her gown.

And –

At these words she turned back her ermine cuffs with a gesture both graceful and savage, and lashed me across the back. I shuddered as the whip cut into my flesh like a knife.

'Well, how do you like that?' she exclaimed.

The dreadful woman even stops the ravenous hero from eating more than a mouthful of sizzling steak for lunch. He ends up tied to a bedpost and whipped by her Greek boyfriend, while 'Wanda lay on the ottoman, her head in her hand, watching the scene with fiendish curiosity and enjoyment.'

He loved every moment, of course. A sadist is only someone who is terribly nice to a masochist.

Sade like Marx won the world's uncommon honour of founding an 'ism'. Marx too was, out of character, a jovial fellow fond of cigars and women, an esteemed contributor to the New York *Tribune* and author of the unfinished comic novel *Scorpion and Felix*. Sade left an infinitely less baleful legacy.

The mass of men lead lives of quiet copulation, but fantasy is free and perversion indefinable – the Puritans found *any* pleasure obnoxious that contaminated the dutiful act of procreation, though the Victorians confined this depravity to women. 'Manners and morals are an arbitrary affair,' said Sade sensibly.

Sex shops today will sell you a cane for the price of a reasonable bottle of claret, with matching accessories in steel-studded black leather, trade brisk among the over-thirty-fives. Domestic sado-masochism is as popular as tennis.

Many a time did I have to bend over and receive six of the best from his hands on that portion of the anatomy which, I was advised by him and implicitly believed, was specially designed for the purpose. In spite of what modern psychologists assert, I never found this altered my very close and loving relationship with him.

Thus Pamela, daughter of the renowned Lord Chief Justice Goddard, reported shamelessly on family life in *The Times* of 4 April 1977.

'Terror is a horrible pleasure,' the Duc de Choiseul observed to Voltaire at Versailles about the time of Sade's hurtful marriage. The giving and receiving of pain lies as deep in the human psyche as the giving and receiving of love. Sade never did anything to harm anyone, no more than professionals were prepared to be paid for. He had infinite vision where others refused to look. He was the H G Wells of Pope's 'tricks to shew the stretch of human brain, Mere curious pleasure, or ingenious pain.'

4 Why Do People Become Doctors?

I was summoned down to Windsor to see the Queen. As it was 'urgent', I immediately took post horses, and in two hours was in the Castle. I arrived so early that I was ushered into the breakfast-room of the Royal couple. The Queen was suffering from a pain in her knee and she gave me a hint that the presence of the King [William IV] might be dispensed with. According I said, addressing the King, 'Will your Majesty be kind enough to leave the room?'

'Keate,' said he, 'I'm hanged if I go.'

I looked at him for a moment; I then said quietly but firmly, 'Then your Majesty, I'll be hanged if I stay.' When I got to the door of the apartment, the King called me back.

'Keate,' said he, 'I believe you're right; I'll retire. You doctors can do anything, but if a Prime Minister or a Lord Chancellor had presumed to order me out of the room, the next day I should have had to address his successor.'

Robert Keate, in *Doctors by Themselves*

5 What Put Carlyle Off His Food?

Literary life, 5 Cheyne Row, Chelsea during the 1850s.

In the first-floor drawing-room, Jane Baillie Welsh ('Jenny') Carlyle, vivacious, charming, generous, jet-haired and boyish-figured, fifty, queening it over her *salon*.

Tennyson, Thackeray, Samuel Rogers, John Stuart Mill, the Brownings, Harriet Martineau, Geraldine Jewsbury, hardly room to pass a teacup between them.

Allusions fluttered like butterflies, shafts of wit pinged as regularly as darts in a pub, epigrams flashed as steadily as lighthouses, criticism killed with the neatness of snakebite, weighty quotations were zestfully ingested with the muffins. It was all so gaily contentious, so dazzlingly competitive! And so carefully rehearsed. *Literati* suffer universally from *esprit de l'escalier* going *up*.

Everybody loved Jenny. When she kissed Leigh Hunt, he rushed home and wrote a poem about it.

> Say I'm weary, say I'm sad,
> Say that health and wealth have missed me,
> Say I'm growing old, but add,
> Jenny kissed me.

Thomas Carlyle did not care greatly for Leigh Hunt, who persistently called for supper despite their giving him Scotch porridge.

Up in the attic, frugal, scornful, overbearing, impatient, intolerant, egotistical, choleric Carlyle sat writing *Frederick the Great* in a self-designed room with double walls, no windows and a skylight, cost £170. He had started writing *Cromwell* downstairs, but the young lady next door took up the piano, practising for hours and hours on end. Carlyle was as sensitive to noise as a bat.

The man who doth bestride this narrow literary world like a Colossus suffered from his stomach.

It was as if a rat was gnawing at my stomach...a gnawing pain over all the organs of digestion, especially in the pit of the left side of the stomach...the accursed hag, dyspepsia, had got me bitted and bridled, and was ever striving to make my waking, living day a thing of ghastly nightmare. I resisted what I could; never did yield or surrender to her. One could not call it hope, but only desperate obstinacy that animated me – obstinacy as of ten mules.

He also had 'rebellion of the intestines' with stools of 'pipe-clay state', he was 'dull, stupid and unable to work' from constipation. And insomnia –

a prey to nameless struggles and miseries, which have yet a kind of horror in them to my thoughts, three weeks without any kind of sleep, from impossibility to be free from noise...sick with sleeplessness, nervous, bilious, splenetic...it is strange how one gets habituated to sickness... I fight with dullness and bile in the forenoons as of old... I was wasted and fretted to a thread. My tongue, let me drink as I would, continued as dry as charcoal.

His mind was shot with 'black streaked lightning', he felt fire rushing through him, and his head was full of air. It all started as a teenager and persisted until he died in 1881, aged eighty-five. The man of letters suffers symptoms far severer than the one in the street.

Treatment was unavailing. A medical 'long hairy-eared jackass' knocked him off smoking. Queen Victoria's physician, Sir Richard Quain, Bart., put him on chalk and mercury, diagnosing 'that he was particularly fond of a very nasty gingerbread'. He tried changing his dinner-hour, bathing at Dover, taking the Malvern waters with Dr Gully of the Bravo case. (Bravo's wife was Gully's mistress, barrister Bravo killed her and himself.)

Carlyle lived two months with 'Stomach Curer' Bedams in Birmingham 'I have been bephysicked and bedrugged, I have swallowed about two stouppels of castor oil since I came hither: unless I dose myself with that oil of sorrow I cannot get along at all.' He decided, 'Of all the sons of Adam, men of medicine are the most unprofitable,' and work 'was the grand cure of all the maladies and miseries that ever beset mankind'. (The philosopher got it wrong, he could start working only when emerging from his bouts of depression.) His elder brother John was a doctor, but they probably avoided each other professionally through mutual prudence.

Thomas and Jenny married in Dumfriesshire, Scotland, in 1826. He was thirty, she twenty-five. She put it off for eighteen months, because he could not keep her in the manner to which she was accustomed. 'I love you and I should be the most ungrateful and injudicious of mortals if I did not,' she wrote candidly. 'But I am not *in love* with you; that is to say my love for you is not a passion which overclouds my judgement.'

Jenny was a doctor's daughter descended from John ('monstrous regiment') Knox. She was an opium addict who shocked everyone by smoking cigarettes. She loved her pets – cats, dogs, canaries, hedgehogs, leeches. Off-*salon* she was spiteful, selfish, irksome, rheumatic, bilious, vertigious, depressed and paranoid. Her husband was unsympathetic – 'My dear, I think I never saw you looking more bilious; your face is *green* and your eyes all *bloodshot*.'

They rowed like any other tetchy couple. He knocked her about a bit. 'The blue marks which in a fit of passion he had once inflicted on her arms' entered literature via her diary. Though she made him lovely marmalade, 'pure as liquid amber, in taste and in look almost poetically delicate'.

In the autumn of 1863 Jenny was run over by a hansom, tore a thigh-muscle, was ill for a year. Her doctor suggested the cure of marital separation. At four o'clock on the Saturday afternoon of 21 April 1866, she had a fatal coronary in her new brougham in Hyde Park, just opposite the Achilles statue.

'The great majority of severe neuroses in women have their origin in the marriage bed,' perceived Freud.

The *habitués* of Cheyne Row dropped hints between the aphorisms 'about the nature of the relations between them, that their marriage was not a real marriage, and was only companionship, etc.' He was impotent. It was the buzz of the London clubs. Carlyle heard, and inserted goaded remarks in *Frederick the Great* despising people who pry into the sex lives of their intellectual betters.

The incorrigibly insufferable Frank Harris, editor of the *Fortnightly Review*, friend of Oscar Wilde and Bernard Shaw, dined with Sir Richard Quain in a private room at the Garrick Club in 1887. 'My story, and I make you a present of it,' offered Sir Richard afterwards, relaying his patient Jenny's account of her wedding night.

'I went upstairs, undressed and got into bed: he hadn't even kissed me of his own accord, the whole day! A little later he came up, undressed and got into bed beside me. I expected him to take me in his arms and kiss and caress me. Nothing of the sort, he lay there, jiggling like.'

'I guessed what she meant,' said Quain. 'The poor devil in a blue funk was frigging himself...'

'I thought for some time,' Mrs Carlyle went on. 'One moment I wanted to kiss and caress him; the next moment I felt indignant. Suddenly it occurred to me that in all my hopes and imaginings of a first night I had never got near the reality: silent the man lay there jiggling, jiggling. Suddenly I burst out laughing: it was too wretched! too absurd! At once he got out of bed with one scornful word, "Woman!" and went into the next room: he never came back to my bed.'

Sir Richard threw in a later consultation in Jenny's bedroom.

'I turned the light full on, then put my hand under her dress and with one toss threw it right over her head. I pulled her legs apart, dragged her to the edge of the bed and began inserting the speculum in her vulva: I met an obstacle – I looked – and immediately sprang up. "Why you're a virgo intacta!" '

Such indiscretion! Perhaps Sir Richard had drunk too much port (as a member of the Garrick Club, I painfully admit this distressing possibility). More likely, Frank Harris made it up. He brought a medical student's gusto to his friends' sexual difficulties.

Carlyle confessed his impotence to Harris during a walk in the rain together through Hyde Park after Jenny's death. 'The body part seemed so little to me, I had no idea it could mean much to her. I should have thought it degrading her to imagine that. *Ay di me, ay di me...* ' The words ring true. Anyway, Frank Harris published them in the *English Review* of 1911.

Carlyle was not homosexual. He had – an assumedly unconsummated – affair with Lady Ashburton, one of the banking Barings, from the early 1840s until her death in Paris in the spring of 1857. 'The most queen like woman I have ever known or seen... Her work – call it her grand and noble endurance of want of work – is all done.' Jenny was jealous, particularly when the Carlyles were invited to share her private railway carriage (ex-Queen Victoria) to Edinburgh, and found that the Lady occupied the spacious saloon alone while they occupied the next compartment with the lady's maid.

Novelist Geraldine Jewsbury was writing to the older Jenny, 'I think of you much more than if you were my lover... I cannot express my feelings even to you – vague undefined yearnings to be yours in some way.' Geraldine was Jenny's 'most intimate and confidential friend', to Carlyle's biographer, tall, spare, unmarried donnish Anthony Froude. 'Carlyle was one of those persons who ought never to have married,' was Geraldine's dark remark, illuminated with 'weird and uncanny' details which Froude worked into the biography, bringing trouble.

The row reached the *British Medical Journal*. The professional hero-worshipper Carlyle was hero-worshipped by Sir James Crichton-Browne MD, also of Dumfriesshire. He had four closely printed pages in the *BMJ* of 27 June 1903, castigating Froude's 'bold, filthy, scurrilous assertions'. Of course Carlyle was not impotent – Sir James knew the doctor who adjusted Carlyle's truss, and the sexual apparatus looked as splendidly sound as the surgical one. Sir James Crichton-Browne was the Lord Chancellor's Visitor in Lunacy.

The 'Janeites' discovered from Jenny's published letters a literary genius stifled by a cruel husband. The Cheyne Row circle was less impressed. 'Do you think,' Browning had said about her sarcastic criticism of Keats, 'I cared more about this than for the barking of a little dog?'

Her husband's impotence is equally unmemorable. What put him off his wife put him off his food. Dyspepsia, insomnia, impotence, their common cause is anxiety. Carlyle sat all day in a soundproof, windowless room, fretting dreadfully about the universe and his guts. His might and his misery were both inspired by a severe anxiety neurosis. A psychiatrist would have done him the world of good. But a philosopher's life is better fulfilled by penning *Sartor Resartus* than eating square meals, and any Attic wit worth his salt would rather have written *The French Revolution* than have had a woman.

6 Which is the Best Aphrodisiac?

Louis XV's doctor knew: 'Ah! Sire! Change is the greatest aphrodisiac of all!'

Nancy Mitford, *Madame de Pompadour*

7 Was Dr Barnardo a Medical Waif?

Dr Barnardo was a shifty fellow.

Victorian philanthropy was embodied in a dumpy Jewish Irishman with a bursting-buttoned, grey frock-coat, spats, tall hat, bow tie and substantial watchchain. His starched white cuffs were buttoned to his shirt-sleeves, a spare pair in his pocket to confound grubbiness. He was a rigorous Plymouth Brother, a flamboyant talker, eager orator and avid publicist. He grew deaf in his forties and flourished an ear-trumpet. He had pince-nez and an upswept moustache like Kaiser Bill's.

The doctor was a stickler for correct address. His children's homes were 'Dr Barnardo's, his visiting-cards announced Dr Barnardo, London's huddled and mostly gin-soaked masses murmured respectfully of Dr Barnardo. In 1872 he bought the Citadel of Satan for £4200 – the Edinburgh Castle pub and music-hall alongside the Grand Union Canal in Stepney, reopened as a Working Men's Coffee Place, the bar redecorated with 'WINE IS A MOCKER, STRONG DRINK RAGING MADNESS'. He at once gave orders that staff and customers must always rightly call him 'Doctor'.

Irksomely, he was not a doctor at all.

Twenty-two-year-old Thomas John Barnardo from Dublin, a thoughtful but cheery chap, entered London Hospital Medical School in the Whitechapel Road on his second try in 1867. He took lodgings with Mrs Johnson, a sailor's wife, in a two-up two-down terrace house convenient in Stepney. In 1868 he was writing, 'With God's help I have worked hard, having been enabled to dissect two complete subjects and I think I am as well up as any man of my year.'

Fearing God's enthusiasm did not match his own, he funked the midway examination in anatomy and physiology, passed it a year later, and drifted away from the hospital. He was intolerantly independent, impatient of authority and resentful of others' judgement. These are qualities which make life difficult for a medical student.

The London Hospital's obstruction to his ambitions could be by-passed like any other. In 1875 he wrote to the Dean of the Medical Faculty at the University of Giessen in the Rhineland (est. 1607) –

> I am about to publish a book on our mission work among the destitute children, and wish if possible to have my name on the title page as 'T J Barnardo MD', and therefore shall be glad to know if you can allow me to be examined by your University early in December as my book will be published about Christmas next. If it were necessary I could try to go over to your University for the examination, but should be glad if that could be done by papers sent here. Kindly let me know the subjects of the examination.

Giessen resented its equation with the fabled open-handed Irish institution which provided medical degrees for a fee after a *viva voce* exam over a pint of stout. Barnardo felt he was only regularizing the position. In 1873 he had a congratulatory letter from Dean L D Wichan awarding him a Giessen MD on receipt of the £15 fee. The letter was written in atrocious German, on English writing-paper, and no L D Wichan existed. Barnardo confessed he suspected somebody had forged it.

He insisted that he *had* become MD (Giess.) at St George's Hospital on Hyde Park Corner in February 1872, in a ten-minute bedside examination by a German physician whose name escaped him. St George's was outraged at the suggestion, particularly as *The Times* was simultaneously thundering about owners of forged degrees 'now disporting themselves in their ill-gotten plumage as if the feathers had been stuck in their coats after honourable University competition. Our readers, therefore, must exercise some little caution before accepting the *ipse dixit* of newly fledged Doctors in their neighbourhood.'

Sanctity is scarce, virtue engenders jealousy, the high-minded can be mean-spirited and charities bitterly uncharitable to each other. His rivals in benevolence published *Dr Barnardo's Homes: Startling Revelations*.

They disclosed him as a medical impostor living on a rake-off from the donations, who forged fulsome testimonials from clergymen, beat the children and locked them in cellars, and faked their photographs in rags and postures of misery for the heart-wrenching placards. The door was ever open only in one direction, and parents demanding their offspring back found them already departed to his two favourite destinations of Canada and the Royal Navy. Under the subtitle *The Very Wicked Woman and Her Story*, he enjoyed an immoral relationship with his landlady Mrs Johnson, who awkwardly later went on the streets.

Barnardo disposed of these libels in the Court of the Exchequer. The children's photographs? Routine fundraising. An eighteen-year-old lad was admittedly flogged and kept in a seven-foot-square cell for a week, but he had been insubordinate to the Doctor. The parents who wanted their children returned – only when old enough to earn wages – were incorrigibly drunken and immoral. (He threatened bothersome couples with investigation and exposure of these infamous habits in court under the Vagrant Act.) Anyway, parents were perfectly free to visit their little ones, up to four times a year.

Mrs Johnson was a case of 'sexual hysteria'. He outflanked sceptics of his medical title with a secret expedition to Edinburgh, to pass the finals at Surgeons' Hall and secure a place on the eighteen-year-old medical *Register*. The trip left him depressed, exhausted and sleepless – he was always dreadfully ill after any strain. If the ever-open door was matched by the ever-open pocket, the public probably agreed with *London Opinion* – 'Let us suppose, for the sake of argument, he cleared ten thousand for himself – I for one will – why shouldn't he? His work is true imperialism and the results would be worth far more than ten thousand a year.'

The newly qualified doctor had 4000 children in his care at a time in 112 homes, a quarter of a million in his lifetime. He died of a coronary in 1905 leaving the equivalent of £4 million, and his funeral was Britain's first newsreel.

The tenements, sweatshops, pawnbrokers, and pubs of Whitechapel, black with soot, flaring yellow with gas, noisy with barrel-organs and tinkers' cries, were the pastures of this shepherd so acquisitive for lambs. Every night he rubbed shoulders with the professional girls who in Victorian idiom 'gave soft for hard'.

In the early hours of Tuesday, 7 August 1888, a thirty-five-year-old tart called Martha Turner was found on the stone stairs of a four-storey dwelling-house off Whitechapel High Street, her throat slit, her body perforated with thirty-eight stab wounds. She was the first of seven victims which embedded Jack the Ripper into the language as firmly as John the Baptist. On 29 September, a forty-five-year-old prostitute Elizabeth Stride – a Swede, also known as Long Liz – was found at one in the morning outside the Socialist Working Men's Club by the secretary. This was south of the London Hospital, between Whitechapel High Street and the Edinburgh Castle. The murderer had seemed desirous to make off with her head. She still clutched a packet of cachous.

'I have since visited the mortuary in which were lying the remains of the poor woman Stride,' Barnardo wrote to *The Times* on 6 October 1888. 'I at once recognized her as one of those who stood round me in the kitchen of the common lodging-house on the occasion of my visit last Wednesday week. One poor creature, who had evidently been drinking, exclaimed somewhat bitterly to the following effect: "We're all up to no good, and no one cares what becomes of us. Perhaps some of us will be killed next!..." '

Dr Barnardo did not know that he was already on Scotland Yard's list of suspects. The murderer generally plucked 'a certain organ' from the mutilated woman. This indicated knowledgeable dexterity. On the pavement, in the dark, with speed fearful of a policeman's bull's-eye, it is an outstanding feat of dissection.

Slaughtermen were suspected, perhaps the *shochets* performing ritual slaughter for the East End's myriad Jews. One man in a slaughterhouse leather apron needed police protection (he had the suspicious name of Pizer). But 'a certain organ' in pig and cow is easily accessible. Suspicion fell regretfully upon that exemplar of the middle-class, a doctor, the murderous knives in his conventional black Gladstone. Triumphant policemen were marching men with little black bags into stations all over the country, one was hounded by a mob when his Gladstone dripped blood (liver for his supper).

An American was suspect after writing round London hospitals for a supply of 'certain organs' at £20 a piece. He was publishing a book on it, and intended presenting a specimen with each copy, as book clubs today distribute busts of Dickens. Dr Barnardo was a more satisfactory Ripper. He had dissected *two* complete subjects, he said so himself. He could lurk in the Edinburgh Castle just down the road. He could flit unsuspected round the East End, in familiar frock-coat and top hat, on his assumed errands of mercy.

A more distinguished suspect in the profession was Sir William Gull, physician to the Queen. It was something to do with the Masons. Sir William was seventy-two and had suffered a stroke. Equally lunatic Rippers created by journalists then or since were the Queen's twenty-four-year-old eldest grandson the Duke of Clarence (a story of the Irish, always explosively mischievous towards the British), seventy-eight-year-old Mr Gladstone, Montague Druitt the cricketer, J K Stephen the poet, Walter Sickert the painter, Queen Victoria and the Mad Pork Butcher of Holloway.

Dr Thomas Neil Cream was a better qualified candidate. He was tall, broad, bald as a pumpkin, with a heavy brown moustache and a squint, a graduate of McGill in Canada and St Thomas' Hospital in London, a jolly soul always fashionably dressed with wing-collar and curly-brimmed topper, chewing gum or a cigar, a pack of pornographic photos in his pocket. He could play the zither. In the spirit of Dr Barnardo, he taught in a Presbyterian Sunday school. He loved giving girls strychnine, to die in convulsions.

At nine in the morning of 15 November 1892, Dr Cream was hanged in Newgate Gaol. As hangman Billington slipped the bolts, Cream said, 'I'm Jack *eeeerrrrkkkk*.' To confess seven famously hideous murders while being hanged for four more is the ultimate in vanity.

The Ripper's murders had stopped in November 1888. He may have committed suicide. He may have retired with his memories. He was never Dr Barnardo, who was such an inept doctor and reacted so neurotically to his exams, that he would have been in bed for months after poking a girl's eye out with his umbrella.

8 How Do You Raise Money for Medicine?

Pasteur presents himself at the house of Madame Boucicault, the widow of the owner of Bon Marché. They hesitate to let him in.

'It's an old gentleman,' says the maid.

'Is it the Pasteur of the dog rabies?'

The maid goes to inquire.

'Yes,' says Pasteur.

He comes in. He explains that he is going to found an Institute. Little by little, he becomes animated, clear, eloquent. 'And that is why I have taken on the duty of bothering charitable persons like yourself. The last contribution – '.

'Why, of course!' says Mme Boucicault, as embarrassed as he is.

After a few trivial remarks, she takes her chequebook, signs a cheque and hands it, folded, to Pasteur.

'Thank you, madame!' he says. 'You are too kind.'

He glances at the cheque and bursts into tears. She does too. The cheque was for a million francs.

Jules Renard, *Journal*, 1900

9 Was Napoleon Killed by His Wallpaper?

England's revenge on Napoleon was in giving him the life of a seedy country gentleman.

On 18 June 1815 in the hands of Wellington he met his Waterloo.

The Emperor fled in his carriage, arriving at the Elysée at six in the morning three days later. Paris was in confusion. The mood of the people had changed from *claquer* to *cracher*. A month later he appeared in Rochfort on the Bay of Biscay, on his way to America. The British and Americans had recently ended a two-year war, and he would have made a fashionable curio for President Madison. But the British knew the business of blockade. Landlocked Napoleon wrote to the Prince Regent of England, 'I come, like Themistocles, to seat myself at the hearth of the British people.' They were represented by Captain Maitland of the seventy-four-gun Battle of the Nile veteran *Bellerophon*, where he was piped aboard at ten o'clock on the morning of Saturday, 15 July.

The hearth was cold and waterlogged. Nine days later the *Bellerophon* anchored in Torbay, then was ordered to Plymouth, where fishing boats made fortunes running trips round the Emperor. Everyone in England was trying to decide what to do with him. *The Times* wanted to hang him, as Lloyd George the Kaiser later. Metternich thought that they should send him to the north of Scotland. Talleyrand thought the Azores. Prime Minister Lord Liverpool revived the 1800 idea of St Helena. Napoleon himself expected to become a gentleman farmer ten leagues from London, incognito as 'Colonel Muiron'.

He was allowed three aides-de-camp, a British doctor and twelve servants. Some irritating, liberal-minded London lawyers tried serving a writ of *habeas corpus* on the admiral commanding the Channel fleet. Napoleon was hurried away aboard the more seaworthy seventy-eight-gun *Northumberland*, commanded by Rear-Admiral Sir George Cockburn, who the previous August had burned down the White House.

St Helena in the South Atlantic is some 1200 miles both west of Angola and below the Equator. It is ten miles across, volcanic, ringed by cliffs reaching 2000 feet, a small gap holding the only port, Jamestown. It had been owned by the East India Company since 1651.

We English do not insult. We are masters of the deadlier demoralizing indifference.

When the *Northumberland* anchored on the morning of 15 October no accommodation had been reserved for the ex-Emperor. No one had mentioned he was coming. When the escorting brig *Icarus* arrived with the news five days before, the inhabitants would have been barely more surprised if she had fired an Exocet at the fort. They heard all at once of Elba, Waterloo, the *Bellerophon*, history in instant replay.

The English put Napoleon up at the local pub. He shortly moved in with the Babcomes at The Briars. Two months later, the man who recently had Europe at his disposal ended with the address of Longwood House, good title for a novel by Jane Austen.

This was a sprawling, single-storey, verandahed dwelling four miles six furlongs from Jamestown, with a muddy courtyard, a drawing-room enjoying a brick fireplace, and a billiard-room. Napoleon always had a British orderly officer breathing down his neck. He could wander four miles alone, further if escorted by a British officer, a privilege he refused to entertain. Every surrounding ridge and road had red-coated pickets; with darkness, sentries closed under the windows. Semaphore signals were prepared for flashing messages from peak to peak to Governor Sir Hudson Lowe, three miles five furlongs away at Plantation House. These covered the possibilities from 'All is Well' to 'General Bonaparte is Ill', 'General Bonaparte Has Been Out Longer than Usual', and 'General Bonaparte is Missing'.

'I am an Emperor in my own circle and will be so long as I live,' Napoleon told Sir Hudson angrily. 'You may take my body prisoner but my soul is free.' He was always having rows with the Governor, with no more chance of winning than Caliban against Prospero. He created a pathetically elaborate court ceremonial. He received his visitors in the billiard-room. He lunched with an aide-de-camp, but at eight the butler in black silk breeches announced, 'Your Majesty's dinner is served,' a formal occasion with officers in braided uniforms and their ladies in low-cut gowns. 'A watch should be kept on the consumption of wine, and no bottle should ever be uncorked unless it is needed,' directed the Governor.

The captors lived the life which the British had scattered across the world. They had tea-parties and dinner-parties with the men left to their port. They constructed a rigid Table of Precedence (senior merchants ranked with lieutenant-colonels, junior ones with majors, commission agents were subalterns). Both sides were sustained by scandal. The ravishing wife of Count de Montholon was having it off with a lieutenant called Jackson, the Governor's wife with one called Den Taafe and hitting the bottle as well. The Chaplain was sacked for preaching on the text 'Publicans and harlots go into the kingdom of God before you,' with too pointed reference to the British admiral's mistress.

Napoleon grew fat on the resented regime.

In his energetic prime he had worked eighteen hours a day, dictated fifteen exacting letters and orders daily, had given himself a *crise de nerfs*. 'His Majesty enjoys good health as always,' surgeon Baron Larrey wrote in the bleak Polish winter of 1807. He had a wound in his left thigh (Toulon, 1793). He had dysuria from stones in the bladder – one attack was in 1812, the night before Borodino. He returned from Moscow stouter, sleepier, looking more than his forty-four years. He had syphlophobia and cancerophobia.

Napoleon has been wildly diagnosed with more diseases than Hitler. Gonorrhoea, malaria, epilepsy, neurodermatitis, syphilis, hormonal deficiency – this perhaps rightly, a British doctor observing after his death, 'Indeed the whole body was slender and effeminate. There was scarcely any hair on the body and that of the head was thin, fine and silky. The pubis much resembled the Mons Veneris in Women. The muscles in the chest were small, the shoulders were narrow and the hips wide.' Every Frenchman knows he lost Waterloo only through painful piles.

'He was by temperament robust,' wrote his valet Louis Marchand at St Helena in 1817. Napoleon at Longwood House caught the usual coughs and colds passing round a closed community, suffered the usual aches and pains of corpulent middle-age. In April 1816, his ankles swelled and pitted to pressure, he found riding irksome. This oedema was of local cause – perhaps varicose veins – not a sign of heart failure. Sketches of him in 1817, 1819 and 1820 show a steadily protruding abdomen but a white-stockinged calf and ankle below his breeches as neat as ever peeped beneath a petticoat.

The second week of September 1816 he suffered an attack of diarrhoea and vomiting, bacilliary dysentery conveyed by his food. Early in 1817, his valet reported, 'The Emperor was seized with an attack of dysentry violent enough to alarm us all.' He became seriously ill for six weeks, was left tired, shivery, sleepy and unhungry.

I believe it was not dysentery, but cholera. This was the British Army's enemy in the rear. The 66th Regiment lost a tenth of its troops every year from sickness at St Helena, probably mostly from cholera which they brought from India. Florence Nightingale was having appalling trouble with it at Scutari thirty-seven years later. Napoleon was as lucky to escape with his life as the day in 1796 when the real Colonel Muiron was killed, sheltering him with his body at the Battle of Arcola.

That summer of 1817, he noticed a painful swelling in his right abdomen. He complained of pain under the right ribs and in the right shoulder, cough and spongy gums. He was treated with the mercury salt of calomel and horse-riding. The shoulder pain got worse, he grew irritable and weak. In January 1818 he had dizziness, treated by bleeding. He was beginning to say, 'How good bed is, doctor! I would not exchange its pleasures for all the thrones in the world.'

By July 1820 he was really ill, with stomach pains and nausea, severe pain in his right side. He was treated with enemas and blistering of the arm. By January he could swallow only soup and jelly, by March he took to his bed with vomiting, which in April became violent. Blood appeared, broken down by the stomach juices, the historic 'coffee-grounds' vomit. He developed hiccups, difficulty in breathing, a rapid, irregular pulse, became cold and clammy. The doctors gave him more calomel, three times the normal dose to make sure. On 5 May 1821 he died. 'What will they say of me when I am gone?' he once speculated on world opinion. 'They will say "*Ouf*".' The post-mortem was performed in the billiard-room.

Napoleon's death, like Napoleon's health, was an extension of politics. The French had ascribed his every ill to English malignancy as expressed through Governor Lowe, isolating him in a damp house on a bleak plateau on an island with an atrociously insalubrious climate. 'My death is premature. I have been assassinated by the English oligarchy and its hired murderer,' said the patient in his will. A procession of four English doctors was appointed, dismissed, even court-martialled, according to their support of the sufferer's view. He expected little better. He once observed to his physician Baron Desgenettes, 'Medicine is the science of murderers.' ('How would you define the science of conquerors?' Desgenettes replied.)

The French accused the English of killing him with arsenic. It was still the age when no person of importance died unexpectedly, but was poisoned.

Captain Thomas Poppleton of the 53rd was the first orderly officer at Longwood House, hit it off with his charge, became the only Englishman ever invited to dine. On 27 July 1817 he was posted, after accepting a gold snuff-box containing a lock of Napoleon's hair, contrary to King's Regulations. On 4 July Rear-Admiral Sir Pultney Malcolm, another of Napoleon's few English friends – and so one of the Governor's many enemies – sailed for home with his wife. She had been given a Sèvres cup and saucer, he a lock of the ex-Emperor's hair. Later there was a lot of it about, his head being shaved after death.

One hundred and forty-five years later, hair claimed to be Napoleon's was analysed by the University of Glasgow and found to contain 10.38 parts per million of arsenic. This is twenty times today's normal level. Arsenic encroaches into every diet, particularly in seafood and vegetables from arsenical soil. In Napoleon's day, arsenic was a common ingredient of medicines and a common contaminant of the antimony salts administered to him as tartar emetic. A second lock of hair also assumed to come from St Helena had a normal arsenic content but a raised antimony level.

On 16 October 1816, aide-de-camp the Count Las Cases stealthily pocketed a lock which fell at his feet while Napoleon was having a haircut from his footman (*Le Petit Tondu* liked it sheared at the back). These hairs became a possession of the Troubetzkoy family, who in 1978 sent them to Glasgow University for analysis.

The snips were thin, reddish, and an inch long, more likely genuine Napoleonic hair than the earlier specimens. The arsenic reached 30.4 parts per million, sixty times today's normal. The chemists compared this with hair cherished in contemporary lockets, which had eight times present levels. And with hair from modern patients over-dosed with arsenic through therapy or attempted suicide, which reached 150 parts per million.

Hair preserved with added arsenic has sensationally high concentrations. Hair dressed with arsenic tonics is contaminated evenly. By cutting the hair in tiny lengths representing a week's growth, the chemists proved that it was contaminated by swallowed arsenic, and dated the rise and fall of Napoleon's weekly arsenic intake. This varied from 11 to 18 parts per million, and matched his periods of recorded illness in 1816. I suspect the arsenic came from the cures rather than the cause of his sickness.

On 25 May 1980, chemist David Jones from Newcastle upon Tyne broadcast about arsenic vapours rising from nineteenth-century wallpaper. Vivid 'Scheele's green' was created in Sweden in 1775 from copper arsenite, by 1815 was recognized as poisonous and liable to give the room's occupants stomach upsets. In 1893 Italian biochemist Gosio discovered that the paper was only dangerous when wet. A mould must get at the arsenic and turn it into poison gas, arsenic trimethyl.

To Dr Jones' surprise, a lady in Norfolk produced a book with a scrap of wallpaper labelled 'This small piece of paper was taken off the wall of the room in which the spirit of Napoleon returned to God who gave it.' The paper was beige flock with a green-and-brown rosette pattern. Though faded, it matched the paper in the Longwood House drawing-room where Napoleon was moved for his last week on earth. Longwood

House was so damp that its wallpaper rotted off, and needed rehanging in 1819.

Glasgow University analysed the fragment with sophisticated x-ray fluorescence spectroscopy. Estimating the density of rosettes on the paper gave its arsenic content as 0.12 grammes per square metre. Nobody knew if this made wallpaper murderous. Lord Armstrong's stately home in Northumberland was currently being stripped of Victorian wallpaper, the lady steaming it off suffering mysterious stomach ills. Glasgow analysed it and discovered that his Lordship stood fifty times the risk of being poisoned by his wallpaper than had Napoleon.

Dr C R Sanger of St Louis investigated in 1893 twenty cases of wallpaper poisoning, all achieved by a half to a tenth of Napoleon's dosage. He added the subtlety that the lower the arsenic the more flourishing its jackal, mould. The *New Scientist* had its joke – 'Was this a case of the killer being hung before the victim's demise?' After World War II, US ambassador Clare Luce was having the same trouble with her bedroom paper in Rome.

Napoleon's terminal doctor was a fellow-Corsican, Francesco Antommarchi, sent out by Napoleon's mother. Unluckily for the patient but luckily for posterity, he was an anatomist trained at Pisa. 'I would give him my horse to dissect, but I would not trust him with the cure of my own foot,' assessed the sufferer.

Antommarchi was incontestably the man for the post mortem, assisted by seven British doctors from a Franco-British audience of seventeen. They started at 2.30 the next afternoon. They discovered:

1 The body was fat, an inch thick over the breastbone, one and a half inches over the abdomen.
2 The left lung had healed pleurisy.
3 There was some clear fluid in the pleural sacs surrounding each lung.
4 The left side of the liver was abnormally stuck to the undersurface of the horizontal muscular diaphragm, which separates chest from abdomen.
5 The liver was stuck to the upper edge of the stomach, its lesser curvature.

6 The stomach was distended and filled with broken-down blood. An ulcer extended almost the entire length of its upper edge. The stomach lining was hardened, especially towards the pylorus which leads on to the gut.

7 A hole large enough for a little finger had perforated the stomach wall near the pylorus. The stomach here was stuck firmly to the liver.

8 The liver was enlarged.

9 The other abdominal organs were normal, the gut full of gas.

10 The lungs were normal.

11 The heart was normal. Napoleon wished that his heart should be pickled and dispatched to his second wife, the Archduchess Maria Louise of Austria. Instead, it was taken by a British doctor, who kept it in his washbasin overnight, where the rats got at it.

Napoleon is assumed to have died of stomach cancer. His father Charles Bonaparte did, aged thirty-eight. Antommarchi's post-mortem report mentions 'a very extensive cancerous ulcer'.

I venture a second opinion. Antommarchi's anatomy was sound, but post-mortems in 1821 were sketchy in technique and knowledge.

No fat men die from cancer of the stomach. Napoleon had a non-malignant peptic ulcer. There was no sign of expected secondary cancerous growths. Most cancers of the stomach arise at either end, non-malignant ulcer is usually along the lesser curvature, like Napoleon's. Peptic ulcers perforate the stomach wall. Cancerous ulcers are shallow and do not. Peptic ulcers seldom become cancerous ones. They can bring thickening of the stomach lining, distinguishable from the infiltration of cancerous cells only under the microscope.

Napoleon's ulcer accounted for his abdominal pain, the liver's attachment to the diaphragm for his shoulder pain. His 'painful swelling' was his flaccid, distended stomach. His ulcer probably perforated the stomach wall when he became severely ill in July 1820. The normal inflammatory reaction glued the hole to the liver, preventing speedy death from the seepage of stomach contents through the whole abdominal cavity. His stomach dilated through narrowing of the pylorus. The bleeding and vomiting disrupted the balance of his bodily chemistry. Perhaps the stuck-down ulcer leaked. He died in shock.

The alternative notion that Napoleon died from an amoebic abscess is improbable. The invisible *Entamoeba histolytica* in drinking water first infects the bowel. Specimens displaying this condition, reputed to have been plucked from Napoleon's corpse, were in the museum of the Royal College of Surgeons in London. The evidence was unfortunately destroyed by Europe's later conqueror. The amoeba grows a cyst in the liver which may rupture into the lungs or the abdominal cavity, but for such devastating effect upon Napoleon it would have been too large for Antommarchi to miss.

Napoleon was not killed by his enemies, official or personal (Count de Montholon had two million francs coming from Napoleon's will). It is as impossible to die from the weather as from ennui, and he offered no signs of arsenic poisoning in life or death. In chronic arsenic poisoning the vomiting and diarrhoea are accompanied by laryngitis, smarting eyes, eczema, skin pigmentation, numbness and wasting of the arms and legs from neuritis. Death comes from heart failure and Napoleon's heart was fine.

He was buried in St Helena, sharing that week the same clerk's copperplate script in the parish register with six British soldiers. When he was exhumed in 1840, arsenic was suspected from the lifelike preservation. This action of arsenic is a myth. The body was sealed like a ham in a tin coffin, within a wood coffin within a lead coffin within another wood coffin, all sunk in cement. The French could always dig him up and have another look, but it would interfere with the tourists.

Napoleon would have died anywhere from the illness he bore in 1821. He died miserably in a remote British colony because he had antagonized the British. Perhaps his nephew had this in mind when he later sucked up to them. 'Napoleon III did no better with the British alliance than his uncle had done without it,' decided A J P Taylor, 'unless it is better to die in Chislehurst than at St Helena.'

10 What Makes Us Different from Animals?

The desire to take medicine is perhaps the greatest feature that distinguishes man from animals.

Sir William Osler, Bart, MD
Professor of Medicine at Montreal,
Philadelphia, Baltimore and Oxford

11 Did Hitler Need Glasses?

Examination of the patient

Age:	34
Height:	1.76 m
Weight:	76 kg
Pulse rate:	72/min.
Blood pressure:	Somewhat raised, 143/90. Systolic reaches 200 when excited.
Dentition:	Poor. Many cavities indicating long-standing neglect. Lower left first and third molars and right first molar missing.

Nasal septum deviated to right. Tenderness over maxillary and frontal sinuses. Post-nasal drip.

Heart and lungs:	Normal
Abdomen:	Normal
Nervous system:	Normal
Urogenital system:	Right testicle only present. No evidence of an undescended testicle in left inguinal canal.
Urine:	Normal

Patch of eczema over left shin. Scar left thigh (shrapnel wound, Somme, 7.10.15). Pustules and scars of boils on back of neck.

Psychiatric condition:	Normal

Patient complaining of pain in right shoulder, incurred in fall to escape police gunfire. Some limitation of movement, but no evidence of fracture or dislocation.

Performed in November 1923. Hitler was in Munich Gaol, passed fit to stand trial for treason.

On 1 April 1924, he got five years, but was freed for Christmas. He passed the sentence writing *Mein Kampf,* an illuminating book punctuated with admiration for the English and contempt for the Germans. His stiff shoulder troubled him for two more years (it was his saluting arm). Six more, he was ruler of Germany. 'Everything I say and do is history.' he informed onlookers. A superman must be blandly superior to ordinary man's agreeable shortcomings. Avoiding meat is little inconvenience, abstaining from alcohol and tobacco commonplace (Hitler liked the occasional beer), disdaining family life possibly a pleasure, renouncing sex may be discreetly camouflaged. *But you can never be ill.*

When forty-three-year-old Hitler was reluctantly made Reichschancellor by eighty-five-year-old President von Hindenburg, he began suffering from abdominal pain after eating. Hitler was a difficult patient. For one thing, he refused to take his clothes off. Dr Karl Brandt (we hanged him in 1947) suggested a full investigation. Unthinkable. Even by military doctors in a barracks hospital. You did not see through the Führer with x-rays. Hitler treated himself with a diet of rusks, honey and yogurt, and Dr Koester's Antigas Pills. It probably helped with his weight. 'Imagine the leader of the Germans with a pot belly!' he once remarked to Speer, aghast.

Three years later the world's greatest orator grew hoarse, a disaster worse than Beethoven growing deaf. It was speedily reversed on 23 May 1936 by Berlin throat man Dr Karl von Eiken, who attended the Chancellor's apartments and removed from the right vocal chord, under local anaesthetic, a benign polyp a centimetre across. (It recurred on 22 November 1944, by then the Americans were in Aachen.)

In 1936 Hitler's photographer Heinrich Hoffmann felt necessitated to attend the fashionable Berlin clap-doctor, Theo Morell. Ex-ship's surgeon Morell was forty-nine, moon-faced and moon-bodied, hair plastered over balding dome, with pale-rimmed glasses and three gold rings on his left hand. He had qualified in Munich, and won neither a distinguished degree nor a degree of distinction. Taking a consulting-room with a fashionable address, he established himself as a suave and comforting practitioner of minor and meaningless medicine.

Our Morells are eternal. They practise in Harley Street, uptown East Side, the *premier arrondissement*. They attract patients from showbusiness, politics, boardrooms and fashionable society who feel uneasy in the severe and inescapably belittling presence of an austerely efficient doctor, who might suggest something unpleasant.

These doctors exist by instantly passing anything they are doubtful of diagnosing or treating to someone who can. They apply to trivial or imaginary illnesses therapy often valueless or eccentric but harmless. They are cautious. They are largely honest, often with themselves. They are useful, necessary practitioners for such discriminating patients. The steely hand of skill is applied in the velvet glove of subservience, like a trusted courtier. Axel Munthe was one, before he went to Capri to write *The Story of San Michele*.

Dr Morell specialized in venereology, sexual disorders, obesity, insomnia, depression. His standard remedy was live bacteria from the faeces of a Bulgarian peasant, swallowed daily in red capsules. He gave some to Hitler. It worked like a charm. The dyspeptic patient was ecstatic. The doctor was brilliant, with exactly the right bedside manner for Führers. He made Morell his *Leibarzt*, personal physician. Morell became a professor and had a lovely uniform with gold serpents on the collar. Hitler went on taking the capsules, two a day until 1943. Everything he said and did for those cataclysmic seven years was performed with Bulgarian peasant poos inside him.

Hitler lived a healthy life. He had jaundice for a week in 1944. During Stalingrad and El Alamein he developed tremor of the left arm, spreading by D-Day to his left leg, which he stopped by jamming his foot round his chair-leg. The shakes were 'a barometer of his excitement', said Albert Speer – all in the mind, *mein Führer*. Parkinsonism, strokes, syphilis are diagnoses pinned to him undeservedly. On 20 July 1944 he suffered ruptured eardrums and burns when they tried to blow him up in East Prussia. A wound the size of a pea in his right hand, which turned septic after ten days, was treated with the new wonder drug penicillin.

The Germans knew of this British discovery because it was all in the *Lancet*, and ampoules of penicillin were captured by the Afrika Korps. The mould was grown in the Hamma pharmaceutical works near Hamburg. Morell had bought the factory with his fees from treating everyone important in Germany. Hamma also made vitamin pills and louse deterrent to prevent typhus, both equally ineffective. 'It would be an inconceivable tragedy if anything should happen to Morell. I could no longer live without him,' Hitler was saying.

Morell took Hitler's electrocardiograms after 1942, wisely sending them to cardiologist Dr Karl Weber for interpretation. The last, made on 24 September 1944, shows impairment of the coronary blood-flow and changes from high blood pressure. American doctors knew this, because they got their hands on the ECG tracings after the war.

Hitler used his improved fortunes to repair the teeth that snarled at the world. He went to Professor Dr Blaschke and Frau Dr Kathe Heusermann for a gold bridge joining nine upper teeth, pinned into the second left and second right incisor, and ten artificial teeth in the lower jaw (four gold), with gold capping and binding. The Russian doctors knew this, because they still have them in a jar somewhere in Moscow.

Morell gave his medicaments like most German doctors by injection. There is generally no reason, except to impress the patient with a painful pinprick that he is getting something worth while. Mussolini's top *Fascisti* would similarly if more comfortably be receiving theirs by suppository. Every other day, Dr Morell injected 4.4 millilitres of vitamins into the Führer's bum. The rate increased to five injections daily. Herr Reich Injection Minister, Goering called him, in his jolly way. Nobody knew what was in them. 'A mixture specially compounded for the Führer,' said Morell arcanely.

'Again it was wonderful the way Morell has helped me,' Hitler enthused to Mussolini in the summer of 1944. 'I was completely exhausted and after his injection I felt fresh again. If it hadn't been for him!' The reason for the efficacy of the treatment was Morell lacing the vitamins with amphetamine. From Germany's reoccupation of the Rhineland to the eve of her unconditional surrender, Hitler was high on speed. When he shouted at his generals for three hours on end in December 1942, people began to notice it.

Man in his forties catches his first blurred glimpse of eternity. He holds his daily paper further away, decides they print modern telephone books badly, complains that the figures are wearing away on his watch. His body has begun to degenerate as one day it will rot, starting with the eyes. He needs glasses.

Hitler's eyes, like Hitler's will, have assumed superhuman qualities. Goebbels murmured, 'Those large blue eyes, like stars.' A schoolfriend from Linz remembered, 'Never in my life have I seen any other person whose appearance – how shall I put it? – was so completely dominated by the eyes.'

Franz von Papen – gentleman showjumper, expelled from Washington in World War I for trying to blow up the railroads, Chancellor of a 'barons' cabinet' whose political contortions vaulted Hitler to power, and who got away with everything at Nuremberg – found him 'curiously unimpressive, the complete *petit-bourgeois*. His demeanour was modest and polite, and although I had heard much about the magnetic quality of his eyes, I do not remember being impressed by them.' British Foreign Minister Anthony Eden thought he had thyrotoxicosis.

On the night of 13 October 1918, runner Hitler of the List Regiment was caught by British gas outside Ypres. I stumbled back with burning eyes,' he told his readers in *Mein Kampf*, 'taking with me my last report of the war. A few hours later, my eyes turned into glowing coals. It had grown dark around me.'

For him the war was over, the wound entered German history. Professor Wilmanns, head of psychiatry at Heidelberg, chief military psychiatrist for the State of Baden during World War I, revealed that his patient Corporal Hitler was not blinded by gas but hysterical after a near-miss by a shell, and when he later saw the Virgin Mary was put under arrest.

In the late 1930s, Hitler was fitted with a pair of steel-rimmed glasses for presbyopia. It was a state secret, comparable with the strength of the Luftwaffe and the tonnage of the pocket battleship *Graf Spee*. Photographs of the bespectacled Hitler were *streng verboten*. His moment of triumph at

3.55 on the morning of 15 March 1939, countersigning President Emil Hácha's surrender of Czechoslovakia, on a marble inlaid table amid uniforms in his vulgarly marbled new Chancellery, was photographed by Heinrich Hoffmann. The negative was scored through because the Führer had his specs on. (Hácha had collapsed during the night's browbeating, disturbing Hitler that he had murdered the sixty-six-year-old cardiac invalid, which the world might think a shade much, even for the Nazis. But he revived instantly with one of Dr Morell's injections.)

As Hitler could not memorize an hour-long diatribe, a typewriter was built with huge letters, the *Führerschrift*. (It was later used by Marshal Zhukov's staff to inform Stalin that Hitler was dead.) He had no electronically operated plastic screens which permit modern statesmen to deliver orations even if as blind as Mr Magoo. Nor contact lenses, though the danger of their popping out during a frenzied passage, his black-uniformed SS bodyguard on hands and knees searching the floodlit dais at a Nuremberg rally, would have halted his career like appearing unexpectedly with his moustache shaved off.

In February 1945 Hitler needed stronger glasses, and was prescribed a pair with dark horn rims. In the Führerbunker under the Berlin Chancellery, at 8.00 on the evening of 1 May 1945, Goebbels handed them to the Deputy-Gauleiter Schact as he prepared to break out – 'Take this as a memento. These are the glasses the Führer used to wear.' Hitler and his bride Eva were dead, their bodies burned to preclude exhibition in a Russian waxworks. Their dog Blondi was dead too, for good measure.

Within the hour, Goebbels had Hitler's doctor Ludwig Stumpfegger (Morell had scampered to Bad Reichenhall and the Americans) inject his six children, between the ages of four and twelve, with morphine. Once they were insensible, Magda Goebbels crushed cyanide capsules between their teeth before taking cyanide with her husband. The doctor had urged that the children be put under protection of the Red Cross. Father replied, 'That is not possible. After all, they are the children of Goebbels.'

Young Gudrun Himmler is today a Munich housewife. Twelve-year-old Helga Goebbels ended on a Russian post-mortem table, photographed with her chin gripped in the rubber glove of a broad-aproned Red Army pathologist, the post-mortem report recording her light blue nightie trimmed with lace and her nine-year-old brother Helmut's blue and red flowered pyjamas. Anyone inclined to restrict free speech – politician or trades unionist – should know the enormity of the sacrifice he is helping to justify.

Mussolini was never seen in glasses, nor Idi Amin nor the Peróns. Comrade Andropov and Herr Himmler do not count, they wear glasses all the time. Sir Austen Chamberlain, British Foreign Secretary of the 1920s did better by intimidating foreign diplomats through a monocle.

Franklin D Roosevelt often surveyed good-humouredly through pince-nez the world he was pocketing for America. Charles de Gaulle sometimes looked down through demi-lunes upon a Europe everywhere inferior to France. Winston Churchill, reading about blood, toil, tears and sweat in his half-moons, regularly appeared a cuddlesome warlord. Mrs Thatcher softens the Iron Lady with pink-rimmed plastic ones.

Her Majesty Queen Elizabeth II, robed, in the House of Lords, facing her supreme legislature of Lords and Commons, amid her great officers of State, tucks a pair of gold-rimmed half eye glasses under her crown and reads the Queen's speech from the throne without a second thought. She is secure in a line of kings and queens barely broken since AD 827. The ruler who must fear ridicule must fear for himself.

PART TWO

Mysterious Addictions

12 How on Earth Do You Do Female Circumcision?

> There's a divinity which shapes our ends,
> Rough-hew them how we will

was Shakespeare's dour comment on male circumcision.

The United States is suffering a pandemic of it. Almost ninety per cent of the two million boys born there every year are afflicted shortly after birth. The silent scourge provokes neither outrage from the press, the fury of Congress nor action by the President. Circumcision is more simply and safely preventable than other childish conditions like whooping cough, measles or diphtheria. It squanders doctors' and nurses' time, and the parents' equally precious savings. Luckily, the mortality is trivial.

Male circumcision has been eliminated in Scandinavia, like smallpox. The epidemic in Britain has been curbed. Go to Rochdale in Lancashire, and you will find only ten per cent of the schoolboys circumcised, the *British Medical Journal* says so. This was the earliest achievement of our National Health Service. Babies with cardiac defects are repaired free of charge, but the medical agrees with the legal profession *de minimis non curat lex*. Infant circumcision is a luxury you pay for.

During the pre-NHS 1930s, circumcision was as fashionable among the British middle class as confirmation. Breech deliveries were said to be popular with both obstetrician and anaesthetist, a boy assuring them early in the birth of 'a couple of guineas next week for the circ'.

The rational needs for male circumcision are negligible. 'Surgeons and urologists in Britain know that many men conceal a dirty mess beneath the foreskin,' the *BMJ* admits. But the foreskin becomes freely mobile in infancy, with the absorption of fine fibrous connections to the glans. The operation prevents cancer of neither the man's penis nor his wife's cervix. The complications run from skinning the organ like a grape to sizzling it away completely with the red-hot diathermy. Circumcision for the prevention of adolescent urinary obstruction – the 'pinhole meatus' – is comparable to forestalling bunions by amputation of the baby's toes. Freud thought that it is all to do with the father wanting to castrate his sons, to show who is boss.

Female circumcision is a paradox more difficult to grasp than the male menopause.

The Egyptians were doing it in 20 BC, Strabo had it in his *Geographica*. They were still at it when James Bruce was looking for the source of the Nile in 1770. Sir Richard Burton appended 'Certain Peculiar Customs' to *First Footsteps in East Africa* in 1856, but his horrified publisher cut it out, even written in Latin. In the 1950s it was a routine operation among the Kikuyu in Kenya. It is being performed still in Kenya, Zaïre, Mali, Sudan and Harley Street, and the House of Lords debated it in 1983.

Some 75 million women have had the operation, which is best done between the ages of ten and fourteen. The African patients' chests are painted with white zig-zags. their faces circled with dotted lines which run down their noses. They make themselves lovely fancy hats. The surgeon is either man or woman, if impressively aged. There is pre-operative singing and dancing, then they disappear into the jungle.

A young man lies on the ground, grasping the arms of the patient who is spread-eagled across his stomach, his thighs the operating table, leafy branches the sterile towels. Assistants prise apart the child's legs by the ankles, the surgeon plucks clitoris and inner labia minora in his fingers and slices them off like the comb of a fighting cock.

The instrument is a kitchen knife or a sliver of glass. Profuse haemorrhage from a wound running between pubis and anus is treated with the application of white chicken feathers, or suturing with thorns and ants' jaws. The patient's legs are bound together, she convalesces for a month in a lonely hut in the care of another old woman. Her soft and sensitive organs heal with tough fibrous tissue, a matchstick inserted to prevent the mess scarring over completely. When she has babies – six is the average – the inevitable tears become even harder tissue, until the woman carries between her legs something resembling a pack-saddle.

There is no anaesthetist.

The clinical reason for the operation is making the girl less sexy, so less likely to prowl when the property of a husband. Some psychologists maintain that it forces a switch from clitoroidal to vaginal sexuality, though they do not talk of this much in the mud-huts round Mount Kenya. Its real reason

requires the understanding of a very important fact in the tribal psychology of the Kikuyu – namely that this operation is still regarded as the very essence of an institution which has enormous educational, social, moral and religious implications quite apart from the operation itself. For the present, it is impossible for a member of the tribe to imagine an initiation without clitoroidectomy.

This advocation was so fiercely pressed by a Kenyan student at the London School of Economics in 1935 that an argument with anthropologist L S B Leakey ended with shouting across the lecture-room, to the puzzlement of the seminar. As the student was Jomo Kenyatta, he must have known what he was talking about.

Female circumcision was already providing a fashionable *frisson* at Mayfair dinner-tables. It was publicly abhorrent to the medical missionaries and the Duchess of Atholl, with whom the British Medical Association and the World Health Organization have now aligned themselves. Also the Women's Committee of the Greater London Council, with greater horror. Kenyatta's successor President Arap Moi banned the operation (ineffectually). The Kikuyu can now afford air fares. European gynaecologists are being importuned to perform the same surgery, if more tidily.

They face the ancient problem of the qualified abortionist – if they refuse, the patient turns to the back streets. In 1982, an infant bled to death in a Paris suburb, after operation by an old woman flown from Africa. Some females suffering from the fashionable neurosis about their rights demand why the hidebound West dare interfere with the traditions, beliefs and sparse physical pleasures of the Third World.

'Compare breast feeding. Once we were made to feel like animals if we breast-fed our children. Now everyone is doing it,' a Nigerian lady author argues with Mad Hatter's logic. How much luckier are the girls of Dahomey in their sexual initiation. They gather in a compound every sundown for a couple of years to massage each other's vulvas. The lady in charge of the class applies ants as stimulation.

Female circumcision proclaims an African girl's sexual maturity, her adult membership of the tribe. We are as savagely addicted to our own puberty rite. With enjoyable condescension and amiable contempt, the mature take delight in forcing the young into a period of pitiable public ignominy, redeemed only by the exuberance of their congratulations when the arduous ceremony is completed. Thank God for the driving test. Women of the West rejoice, you have nothing to lose but your L-plates.

13 Why Does Port Cause Gout?

> At last the happy truth is out –
> Port wine is not the cause of gout;
> Far more responsible for pain
> Are kidneys, liver, sweetbread, brain –
> The clubman should by any means
> Avoid anchovies and sardines,
> And citizens of every sort
> Owe some apology to Port!
>
> A P Herbert in *Punch*
> (by kind permission of Lady Herbert)

(Gout is a disease of metabolism akin to diabetes. It is triggered by the delicious offal listed above. It can occur in a teetotal athletic monk on a diet.)

14 Is Cannibalism Fattening?

At 2.18 on the afternoon of Friday, 13 October 1972, a Uruguayan plane chartered by a rugby football club to fly from Montevideo to Santiago in Chile left its stopover at Mendoza in the Argentine, and an hour later crashed into a snowy valley 12,000 feet up the Andes.

Of the forty men and five women aboard, twenty-nine were dead or to die. Their surgeons were two second-year medical students. Their food was thirteen bars of chocolate and nougat, a packet of biscuits, jam and two tins of mussels. They had some whisky and crème de menthe. Water was abundant, from snow melted by sunlight in aluminium pans fashioned from the plane's seats. After four days, they were hungry. One of the rugger players suggested flippantly eating the two pilots crushed at their controls: 'After all they got us into this mess.'

No sign of rescue. Five days, and anxiety frothed into hysteria. On the Sunday afternoon of 22 October, the twenty-seven still alive decided to eat the eighteen who were not. These were in prime condition, in Nature's deep-freeze. The difficulty of a cutting implement was resolved by adapting a broken glass. The unfamiliar one of where to start was eased by the buttocks of the nearest corpse protruding from the snow.

One of the medical students slivered matchsticks of frozen flesh and defrosted them on the plane's roof in the sun. By nightfall, everyone had helped himself. Nobody wished to know who it was.

Eating People is Wrong! sang Flanders and Swann in the 1950s. But by instinct or on principle?

Since men ate, they ate each other. The same Strabo who exposed female circumcision in Egypt found cannibalism commonplace on the shores of the Caspian Sea and among the Irish. The Conquistadores of the sixteenth century recounted it among the West Indian Caribs, who gave its name. Marco Polo ran across it in China. It was popular until the twentieth century in Africa, South America, New Guinea, Polynesia, Fiji, Sumatra, Australia, New Zealand and among the Red Indians.

There are four incitements to cannibalism among the susceptible.

'The flesh and blood of dead men are commonly eaten and drunk to inspire bravery, wisdom, or other qualities for which the men themselves were remarkable,' teaches *The Golden Bough*.

Of a brave – if sadly ineffective – enemy, eat his liver, seat of his valour. Eat his ears to consume his intelligence. His brow to absorb his doggedness. His testicles to acquire his strength. The ingredients were often economically blended into a *pâté*. Zulu chief Matuana drew vigour from the bile of thirty subjected chiefs (very nasty). It was flattering to the British in 1824, when their Governor of Sierra Leone had his heart consumed by officers of the rebel Ashanti army, the rest of him distributed as rations to the ranks, his bones retained in the regimental mess-hut as sacred relics.

The second encouragement is religion.

'When you die would you not rather be eaten by your own kinsmen than by maggots?' a Peruvian cannibal asked a missionary perfectly reasonably. The Sioux and Brahmins ate boys and girls and sprinkled the fields with their blood, encouraging the gods to stimulate the crops. The Bible agrees, 'Only ye shall not eat the blood; ye shall pour it upon the earth as water' – though respectably referring to roebucks and harts.

Aztec priests in the fifteenth century munched torn-out hearts of young married couples, from the highest motives. The Pawnee Indians were as devotional in 1838, with teenage girls roasted alive. Officers of Jomo Kenyatta's Mau Mau in the 1950s were required to taste the brains, blood and bones of a white man on promotion. When the Black September assassin of the Jordanian prime minister spoke in 1971 of drinking his victim's blood, he meant it.

The third inducement is greed.

Where meat is scarce, man is tastier than monkey. Cookery instructions (*à la Fiji*) are given in the *Methodist Missionary Notes* of 1838.

The victim is kept for some time, and supplied with an abundance of food, that he may become fat. When about to be immolated, he is made to sit on the ground with his feet under his thighs and his hands placed before him. He is then bound so that he cannot move a limb or a joint. In this posture he is placed on stones heated for the occasion (and some of them red-hot hot), and then covered with leaves and earth, to be roasted alive.

A useful culinary hint for the head is coating it with mud and baking separately, as the gypsies do with hedgehogs. He tastes like pork, but is more digestible. A boiling palm-oil enema first renders the meat more succulent.

The best eating is the palms, fingers and toes. The tongues are delicious, and may be drawn out by fish-hooks, sliced off, roasted and enjoyed to merry taunts of 'We're eating your tongues!' at the providers of the feast.

A wayward servant girl in the Fijian royal household was honoured to sit at table with the king while he ate her roasted arm, amputated at the elbow. In Gabon, each progressively dismembered captive could savour the relish of his hot joints being eaten, course by course.

In Fiji 150 years ago, they collected a serving of brains by running a succession of spreadeagled prisoners headfirst against a special braining-stone, before an audience. They are best cooked with sago. One Fijian man was as fond of human flesh as of his wife, and happily combined both tastes. A chief was so gluttonous towards humans that he discovered he had eaten all his tribe, and began tearing at himself: with fatal result.

The Fijians enjoyed feasts of 250 bodies (their only indigenous meat was rats). The accompanying vegetables were yams and small bitter beans. Towards the end of the nineteenth century in Sierra Leone you could buy a hamper of dried human flesh, the chief had his box of salted arms and legs for his friends. Hangchow during the eleventh century was famous for its human-meat restaurants, men and women, adults and children, all creating different *spécialités de la maison.*

A useful spin-off from this gluttony was skulls for reliable cups, population control and flutes from the bones. In Europe, the overrunning

Tartars of the thirteenth century were fond of women. The officers got the girls, the soldiers the stringier matrons.

The fourth reason for cannibalism is compelling necessity.

During Napoleon's retreat from Moscow in 1812, when the *Grande Armée* had no more dead horses to eat, they ate each other. On 5 July 1816, 150 French soldiers and settlers sailing to Senegal aboard the frigate *La Méduse* took to a hastily built raft when she ran aground off West Africa. After a week, the living started eating the dead afloat all round them. They cooked in a cask lined with damp cloths, to prevent burning their boat. Two days later, the fifteen who felt strong enough for survival tipped those who appeared not to be into the sea, to spare the wine ration. You can see it all in the Louvre.

In 1857, half a wagon-train of eighty-four men, women and children survived a winter lost in the Rockies only by eating the other half who did not. In 1901, Peking sent an official to Kwangshui to pacify the natives, but they boiled and ate him instead. In the mid-1920s, two German butchers called Grossmann and Haarmann were separately making a living by selling hot dogs of young women and young men.

In World War II, the British Ministry of Food decided against turning expired bottles from the blood-bank into those succulent northern delicacies, black puddings. British medical officers striving with scanty equipment and few drugs to keep alive their fellow-prisoners of the Japanese, baked human blood into biscuits – but even the starving refused them. 'The much more reduced nourishment in the Nazi concentration camps,' a psychiatrist wrote with professional impassivity, 'led to cannibalism… Only in the last stage before death, does the apathy and the stupor become so severe that the craving for food disappears.' In December 1972, the pilot of a crashed Canadian air-ambulance survived only by eating the nurse.

The rugger team in the Andes acquired a taste for themselves quicker than is customary for *escargots* or *cuisses de grenouilles*. Scrum-half ate full-back, the three-quarters tucked into the forwards. They cooked on more aluminium foil over a fire of Coca-Cola crates. An avalanche on the eighth day augmented the larder by eight. They struggled with unprecedented problems. How soon should they eat their fresh friends? Do you eat your own cousin? Your own sister and mother? The wife of a surviving widower? The ill-effect was diarrhoea.

After six weeks they ran short of handy supplies. They dug for earlier bodies, starting with a mass widdle to melt the snow. Their reward was those killed in the crash being fatter. The diet was intolerable only in its monotony.

At five in the morning of 11 December, an expedition of three left to raise help, with snacks for ten days. When they excitedly found themselves approaching civilization, they roasted their rations and gorged. Next morning, villagers gave them bread and cheese. They shamefully buried their scraps, revolted.

According to the *American Anthropologist*, four pounds a day of live meat would keep a man going through the Ice Age. One fully grown man could feed five others for a week, one-fifth of him a head. The rugby players did not do themselves so well. The sixteen survivors had eight left from twenty-nine corpses, including the two pilots wedged in their seats. Roughly, this represents two bodies a week for their seventy days' isolation, a portion of one-tenth of a man each, half Ice Age rations. They look flourishing enough in the last photographs before their rescue. Had they felt free to indulge with Ice Age gusto, they would assuredly have put on weight.

Is eating people more wrong than Catholics eating chops on Fridays, Hindus beef any day, Jews pork?

'Some additional ideological or emotional stimulus is required to overcome instinctive repugnance to cannibalism,' wrote anthropologist Dr Miller.

'There is probably no instinctive aversion,' wrote anthropologist Dr Spier.

Our instinct of self-preservation is overwhelming, the pavilions of our civilization are flimsy, we do not care to contemplate too deeply whatever prowls in the darkness outside.

The Andes survivors got a bestseller for their pains.

15 Would Another Little Drink Do Us Any Harm?

It is interesting that most of the human race has a reserve of the enzyme necessary to render alcohol harmless to the body – as if nature meant us to drink alcohol, unlike animals to which alcohol is a poison.

BUPA News, 1982

16 Is Smoking Good For Us?

> Sweet, when the morn is grey;
> Sweet, when they've cleared away
> Lunch, and at close of day
> Possibly sweetest

cooed Charles Stuart Calverley's *Ode to Tobacco.*

A century later, this fragrant Virginia haze in a Cambridge don's rooms was prosaically turned into a cloud of poison gas by medical statisticians, neatly correlating an increase in lung cancer with an increase in smoking.

This was the first ringing challenge to the Captain of our Men of Death. Response was muted. Everyone had a grandfather who died at ninety while lighting his third cigarette before breakfast.

'Advice is seldom welcome; and those who want it the most always like it the least,' the Earl of Chesterfield told his son. Londoners in 1854 ridiculed the notion of cholera borne by the water, until Dr John Snow proved it by stealing the handle of the Soho pump (he had the agreeable posthumous honour of a local pub named after him). Americans in 1910 building the Panama Canal laughed at the fancy of deadly yellow fever brought by flimsy mosquitoes. English aristocrats die on the hunting field every season from sporting traditional toppers, not hard hats like farmers. Men prefer looking stupid to the knowing rather than faint-hearted to the general.

The directors of cigarette companies surely sat as shamed as the board of the White Star Line, who failed to provide enough lifeboats for the *Titanic*. They surely contemplated converting their factories to marmalade, expelling their workers to draw the dole in sackcloth and ash.

Luckily, these far-seeing men did nothing of the sort. They preserved the European and American economies, and society as we know it (largely from television).

It took thirty years before chastened tobacco executives complained that national Don't Smoke Days (you chew a raw carrot instead) threatened personal freedom. Or dared to advertise in the London papers with the calm authority of Mr Pecksniff – 'Did you know that over 40% of the adult population smoke and pay £11,500,000 a day in taxes on tobacco?' Otherwise pushing up sales tax by seven per cent and income tax by seventeen per cent more than the straitened British paid for fighting Hitler.

How modest they are!

Did *they* know that (deducting £750,000 a day for National Health treatment of smoking-related cancers, coronaries and chronic bronchitis, a mere speck of ash in the cash) zealously self-sacrificing, patriotic smokers save the country uncountable millions a day in medical and social care for the non-existent elderly?

Britain's lucky working population of 26 million must support as well as themselves a 12 million population of over-sixties, who will increase – as in Europe and the United States – by fifteen per cent in the next forty years. Our Ship of State is ballasted with geriatric slag. We are already down to the gunwales. Another generation, the bottom will fall out and we shall sink.

If our admirably altruistic smokers started younger (average age now twelve), inhaled deeper and indulged oftener, if their benevolent suppliers could advertise on TV, drop those prissy, bleak health warnings, make smoking as vital socially as breathing is physiologically, with luck most of the population would be dead at sixty-five. Each British smoker is admittedly doing his best, helpfully increasing his consumption by twenty-eight per cent in twenty years. He is as usual behind the efficient West German, who has increased his by eighty-six per cent.

This would save the welfare state £12,000,000 yearly in old age pensions, for a start. It would be easier to find a bed in the National Health Service than a seat in the National Theatre. Meals on Wheels would seize up, Age Concern diversify into baby sitting, British Rail charge everybody full fares and show a profit. Hypothermia would vanish from the world, like smallpox, and Florida could go back to the oranges.

Can any government grasp this? Not when they hysterically insist on drivers' seat-belts and cruelly dry up the source of kidney transplants.

The Social Democratic Party was founded in Limehouse in 1981 to break the mould of British politics. The smoking electorate had already done it.

Labour voters dropped two million between the General Elections of 1950 and 1979 because they were all dead. Like doing the football pools and basking in Spain, smoking is largely a working-class pastime. Only twenty-one per cent of British nobs smoke, but fifty-seven per cent of manual workers do, nearly three times as many. In continental Europe, the modern peasantry smoke more than the aristos. American society is classless, but needs both millionaires and truck-drivers, who do the smoking. This is partly through boredom — running a bank is more diverting than digging up Wall Street — partly because the workers find anti-smoking arguments more difficult to grasp than anti-nuclear ones, and partly because workers' tomorrows look after themselves. To raise your life expectancy, raise your social class.

Smoking offers an elegant illustration of women's liberation. In the European Economic Community, women buy forty per cent of the cigarettes and, over the last ten years have increased their mortality from lung cancer by forty-eight per cent. It is a heartening revelation that parents retain their ancient influence over wayward modern children. A child of ten has seen Dad light up 25,000 times before following father's footsteps to an early grave.

'What about cricket, sir?' they puff purple-faced over their vivid scarlet-and-gold striped ties in the pavilion at Lord's.

Indeed, sir!

Our glorious national game, chauvinistically incomprehensible, nurtured by the Men of Hambledon on Broad Halfpenny Down in the

1770s, each match now lasting days on end, between players clothed white as angels and mostly totally immobile, before spectators ripening in the sun on beer and sandwiches…withdrawing cigarette sponsorship would stub it out. Non-smokers are only spoilsports, sir! Already English cricketers are scoffed for protecting their brains with helmets, though for years they have been protecting their testicles with a box, perhaps a realistic sense of values.

World Medicine suggested keeping both cricket and people alive by financing the game with five extra fixtures a season at famous Test Match grounds like Old Trafford, Trent Bridge, Lord's, where a team of eleven selfless smokers would be thrown to the lions.

This is entertainment of 2000 years' guaranteed box office appeal. Only a century ago, a 100,000 crowd would jostle to watch the extinction of only one man, all over in a jiffy, and at eight o'clock in the morning.

The gates would need closing before start of play, the TV fees fantastic. Lion Choc Bars would pay through the nose. The game would be unaffected by rain and bad light, controversial umpiring decisions simplified to thumbs-up or thumbs-down, and no spectators would run on the pitch. The fifty-five smokers eaten while demonstrating their everyday bravery towards the risk of premature death would be *one per cent* – a mere wisp – of the 55,000 unnecessary deaths caused in Britain every year by tobacco.

Smokers are the most blessed of martyrs. Even St Sebastian did not pay for the arrows. They could as philanthropically solve a global problem graver than where to site the missiles.

The world's population is increasing by a million every Monday to Friday – 10,000 an hour, leaving a gap between midnight and 4.00 a.m. for the obstetricians to get some sleep. By the year 2000 there will be 6000 million of us, Population Concern just north of Oxford Circus know it for a fact. Parking will be appalling and supermarket check-outs impossible.

We could abort the unwanted foetuses, but this upsets the Roman Catholics ('an agreement among two or more persons to cause the violent death of an innocent and defenceless human being,' a Spanish bishop put it recently with Inquisitional fire). So does contraception, which is complicated for Third World parents, who tend to slice and eat the condoms. Smoking is anathema to nobody. It is as simple as drawing breath. Heavy smokers under sixty-five die at twice the rate of non-smokers. The United Nations' scattering the world with free cigarettes would restore Nature's balance between sower and reaper.

Tobacco is a cruel addiction. To kill yourself with a car, you need drive fast and far. With alcohol, you must drink deep. A few daily cigarettes can trigger the suicidal pistol.

'Our two main enemies, cancer and ischaemic heart disease, are both essentially avoidable,' Sir Richard Doll told the Royal College of Physicians.

O God, why did you not have Him say, 'But deliver us from ourselves?'

17 Which Book Gives the Best Advice About Dieting?

Talking of a man who was growing very fat, so as to be incommoded with corpulency; he said, 'He eats too much, Sir.' BOSWELL: 'I don't know, Sir; you will see one man fat, who eats moderately, and another lean, who eats a great deal.' JOHNSON: 'Nay, Sir, whatever may be the quantity that a man eats, it is plain that if he is too fat, he has eaten more than he should have done. One man may have a digestion that consumes food better than common; but it is certain that solidity is increased by putting something to it.' BOSWELL: 'But may not solids swell and be distended?' JOHNSON: 'Yes. Sir, they may swell and be distended: but that is not fat.'

Boswell's Life of Johnson, 28 April 1783

PART THREE

Everyday Medical Mysteries

18 Do Doctors Make Good Murderers?

I

Lancaster is a town in north-west England near Morecambe Bay, famous for shrimps. Just south, down the coast, is Blackpool, famous – according to Stanley Holloway's monologue of the 1930s – for fresh air and fun. Lancaster's most popular medical man in those days was Dr Buck Ruxton, practising from a three-storey, stone-faced terrace-house with neat front railings and flowerboxes in a quiet cobbled square.

Dr Buck Ruxton was Buckhtyar Rustomji Ratanji, a *hakim sahib* qualified in Bombay. Mrs Ruxton was Mrs Van Ess. She gave up her husband and her restaurant for the doctor in 1928. In the summer of 1935 she was twenty-nine, he thirty-one, their sex life the well-recognized sequence of angry aggression with a crescendo of copulation. 'I wonder how I could pick a row with you?' Belle Ruxton would ask coyly in the consulting-room.

This technique is superb for circulating the exciting adrenalin but brings a noisy home life. The doctor suffered emotional explosions, with jealous accusations, threats and blows, brandished revolvers and knives at throats. The police had been round twice. Belle had tried to gas herself. The unruly union regularly produced children, aged six, four and two. They were tended by twenty-year-old Mary Rogerson, who lived in that diverting household.

On the Sunday morning of 15 September, the doctor suffered an annoying cut to his right hand while clumsily taking a tin-opener to some peaches for his children's breakfast. It bled profusely, soaking his shirt and suit, towels, sheets, blankets, the curtains, the stair-carpet and underfelt, it stained bath and geyser, the bathroom walls, the chessboard linoleum. He took the children for the day to his friend the dentist, who examined the cut across three fingers, one down to the bone. An oddly savage sort of tin-opener? murmured the dentist. Might he see it? But the doctor in his fury had already thrown it away. Now he must hasten home. He had suddenly decided to have the place redecorated.

Preparation for the decorators entailed tearing up the stair-carpet, so bloodstained from his mishap that he bought a two-gallon can of petrol to burn it in the backyard. But it rained. He gave it and the drenched suit to a lady patient, who used thirty buckets of water and a scrubbing brush without expunging the blood. His daily charlady Mabel washed Mrs Ruxton's white silk nightie because of the bloodstain as big as her hand. Everyone was sorry over the doctor's little accident.

He was breakfasting the children that morning because his wife had driven to see the famous Blackpool illuminations and vanished. So had Mary the nursemaid. He had already informed the police that Belle had bolted to Edinburgh with her lover, a young man from the Town Clerk's office. He had also informed Mary's parents that the girl was 'in trouble', and had been taken by Mrs Ruxton to Edinburgh to be got out of it.

On the Sunday morning a fortnight later, a young lady from Edinburgh on holiday at the Lowland village of Moffat paused on the pretty flint bridge spanning the deep, wooded gully of Gardenholme Linn, and was disconcerted to notice a human arm. The Dumfriesshire Constabulary was summoned. They found seventy pieces of body, including a head wrapped in the *Daily Herald*, the most interesting item ever to appear in that defunct workers' newspaper.

The police had a corpse with spares – three legs, another head wrapped in child's rompers, different feet and legs sharing the same parcel, a uterus and three breasts. The bits had been chopped about and some teeth extracted post-mortem. The limbs were detached the easy way, by cutting through the joints. The energetic dismemberer knew what he was about. The area was known locally as 'The Devil's Beef Tub'.

A doctor cannot abandon his practice, even with a severed hand and a missing wife. The surgery in Lancaster was so busy it became overwhelmed with blood-stained cotton-wool swabs. The patients were beginning to notice insanitary smells. Fires burned continually in the backyard, and the doctor himself had to scrape the soot from the walls with an axe.

Dr Ruxton had been imploring the police all fortnight to find his Belle. Now the newspapers were outrageously linking him with the carnage at Moffat. The publicity was liable to ruin his practice, just as he was trying to raise a loan on it. He was the most miserable man on earth, he told them. He grew excited, burst into tears, begged, 'Can't you publish it in the papers that there's no connection?' The police obliged the doctor.

Other doctors were meanwhile sorting out the bits in Edinburgh. 'I estimated that the dismemberment and mutilation of the two bodies must have taken about eight hours,' said Professor of Forensic Medicine Sir Sydney Smith. 'One can well imagine Ruxton's state of mind with that mass of flesh and bones in his bathroom. It looked sufficiently formidable to me when I first saw it in my laboratory.' They did a double three-dimensional jigsaw, and took clever photographs fitting Mrs Ruxton's skull into a studio portrait wearing her tiara (she was a witless-looking woman with big teeth).

The flesh was cast upon the waters before 19 September, because the flooded Gardenholme Linn had marooned items on the banks. And after 15 September, date of the *Daily Graphic* wrapping a leg and featuring Morecambe's Carnival Queen. It was a special edition for the seaside.

The police traced the doctor through the rompers, Mary's blouse, a sheet matching one on his bed. He had strangled his wife, Mary Rogerson saw him, was hit on the head and her throat cut. Cunning removal of teeth, of Mary's birthmark and squinting eye, of Belle's bunion, only eased identification by attracting notice. He took the bodies one hundred miles to Moffat that same pouring night. (Though his car was clean in the morning, nor revealed to the police a drop of blood. And the neighbours heard nothing.)

Dr Ruxton was arrested in October, tried in March, became hysterical in the witness box, was hanged in May. It is a mystery why any doctor should exhibit such carelessness, which in the more conventional application of his profession would have him struck off for gross negligence. But Dr Ruxton had not even the temperament to be a surgeon.

Madame Tussaud's Waxworks preserves the unmelting fame of medical men only in the Chamber of Horrors. Dr Ruxton consults eternally with Dr Crippen.

The Crippens were American. The doctor came from Coldwater, Michigan, graduated at Cleveland, studied a year at London's Royal Bethlehem Hospital for the Insane, specialized in throats and dentistry, practised in Salt Lake City, St Louis, Toronto, drifted into mail-order patent medicines. This was big business, Edwardian doctors' medicines being equally ineffective. 'Professor' Munyon of Philadelphia paid him $10,000 a year to open a branch in London.

Crippen was slight, balding, heavily moustached, with gold-rimmed glasses and bulging eyes, a sharp dresser in satin-lapelled frock-coat, wing collar and imitation diamond tiepin. He never smoked nor drank, was slightly deaf and henpecked. 'A more humble unassuming little man I have never met,' confessed his professional partner. 'As docile as a kitten,' said his boss. 'One of the nicest men I ever met,' testified his old landlady (on oath).

Like Dr Ruxton's, Dr Crippen's wife was Belle. Belle Elmore was her stage name, her real name was Cora Turner (though *really* it was Kunigunde Mackamatski, her Polish father had a fruit-barrow in Brooklyn). She married Dr Crippen at nineteen when she was living with a man called Lincoln. The doctor's first wife was dead, his son Otto lived in California.

They lived in a semi-detached three-storey house at No. 39 Hilldrop Crescent in the London of gaslight, hansoms and abounding self-confidence. And music halls. Belle fancied herself as a star. She was fat and had no voice, but thought she looked like Marie Lloyd. She made her husband smother her in furs and hang her with jewels (real, not theatrical). She was noisy, pushy, jolly, sociable. As treasurer of the Ladies' Music Hall Guild she enjoyed the twilight of a career which never dawned.

The Guild's office was in Oxford Street, below Dr Crippen's Yale Tooth Specialists. His typist for the mail-order miracle cures was Ethel (Le) Neve, slim, pale, brown-haired, big-eyed, twenty-four. The doctor was forty-seven. They had sex in the afternoons near King's Cross Station.

Belle was a pinchpenny housewife, an enthusiastic home decorator – everything at Hilldrop Crescent was bright pink, down to the bows on the picture corners – an effervescent hostess. On Monday 31 January 1910, the Crippens gave dinner to the Martinetti husband-and-wife comic act. It was freezing. At 1.30 a.m. Belle ordered the doctor through the sleet for a hansom. 'Don't come down, Belle, you'll catch your death!' screeched Clara Martinetti up the front steps.

Two mornings later, Belle was on the boat to America. A letter to the Guild – dictated by her, signed in her absence – divulged a dramatic cable to nurse a sick relative. She resigned as treasurer and enclosed the chequebook. The Guild was affronted. Why had she not paused to say goodbye? They would have gone to the boat train with flowers. Nobody at all had seen Belle since the Martinettis came to dinner. Dr Crippen explained that she was busy packing.

Three weeks later came the Ladies' Guild annual ball at the Criterion in Piccadilly Circus, a function with the social intensity of Mrs Astor's in New York. Dr Crippen took Miss Le Neve in Belle's silk magenta dress, fox fur, gold watch, pearl earrings, diamond ring and familiar brooch like the rising sun. Also a wedding-ring. Eyebrows went up like skyrockets.

A month later the Guild had a telegram, BELLE DIED YESTERDAY AT SIX O'CLOCK. It was dispatched from Victoria Station. The doctor and Ethel were just off for their Easter holiday in Dieppe. An obituary notice appeared in the stage newspaper *Era*, among the advertisements for out-of-work jugglers and trick cyclists. It had happened in California.

Belle had died from double pneumonia after a chill caught on the boat. People were beginning to ask which boat? *La Tourenne*, he replied. Or *La Touvée*. French Line, anyway. No, *La Touraine!* But that was in dry dock. Really? Where in California had she died? Los Angeles. Or San Francisco. Or some other place with a Spanish name. Where was the funeral? She was cremated! Yes, they were very up-to-date over such things in America! Where were the ashes? In the office safe at the Tooth Specialists. Correction.

As a matter of fact, Belle was not dead at all. He had said so only to spare himself scandal. She had absconded (like Dr Ruxton's Belle) with her lover, a song-and-dance man from Chicago.

Scotland Yard arrived at Hilldrop Crescent. Doctor and typist had vanished. They dug up the garden. They dug up the coal-cellar. They found internal organs, bits of muscle and skin, lots of fat. They were fresher than Dr Ruxton's handiwork, though the policemen were permitted to reach constantly from shovel to brandy-bottle. They were encrusted with lime – not *quick*lime, the gravedigger had muddled the two. It was a woman, filleted. No bones. No head. It contained half a grain of the drug hyoscine, a hundred times the safe dose.

Co-interred was a curler with six inches of hair, a lady's lace-trimmed vest and woollen combinations, and the green-and-white flannel pyjamas which Mrs Crippen had bought for the doctor at Jones Bros of Holloway for 17s 9d. Dismemberment of your spouse seems to provoke forgetfulness.

The doctor and Ethel planned their secret escape. It was the most sensational transatlantic crossing until Lindbergh's. They took a slow boat to Canada as father and son. The captain – keen-eyed seadog! – observed the lad had bumps on his chest. The Marconi key dash-dotted. Scotland Yard dispatched an inspector by fast liner. The papers were full of maps with arrows racing across the ocean. The fuss was unnecessary, the Mounties would have done just as well. But steam, the wireless and transvestism were irresistible.

The doctor landed at Liverpool in handcuffs. The inspector thought him a jolly decent little chap. The body was already under the coal when he had rented the house, Dr Crippen explained at the Old Bailey. He had fled only to escape the distressing gossip. He was at a loss over his failure to inquire about the faithless Belle at the shipping offices, or even the local cab-rank.

The defence tried proving that Belle was someone else (they were passing bits of her round the court on an enamel dinner-plate). Top barrister Sir Marshall Hall said *he* would have got weedy womanizer Crippen off with manslaughter, on the excuse of an inadvertent overdose of the sedative hyoscine to dampen Belle's voracious sexual appetite, but he only thought of it afterwards. Dr Crippen was hanged in Pentonville Gaol, just across the Caledonian Cattle Market from home, for atrocious incompetence. It was a mystery why a doctor who successfully persuaded everybody to swallow useless medicines could persuade nobody to swallow the story of a fugitive wife.

Ethel was tried as accessory. Her barrister was F E Smith, 'the cleverest man in the kingdom'. He freed her in one day and one speech. The judge later cavilled at his not making sure of acquittal by calling her as a witness. 'FE' replied, 'I knew what she would say, you did not.'

Ethel Le Neve's life moved her from that north London suburb of Holloway to the south London one of Croydon. When she died there in 1967, the Americans were orbiting the earth. They never discovered Belle's bones and head. A woman's skull made headlines when dug up nearby by builders in 1962. But it was found to be the sort used by medical students, so regrettably inclined to pranks.

II

Dr Edward Pritchard was condemned to death in Glasgow on 7 July 1865, his sentence including the gratuitous aggravation of being 'fed on bread and water only' in the interim.

Like Dr Crippen, like Dr Ruxton, Dr Pritchard was a terribly nice chap. Pious, too. Always handy with a biblical quote. He was forty, tall, bald, sharp-nosed, with a lovely curly brown beard. He had been a naval surgeon, visited Pitcairn Island, lectured on it. He met strong-jawed, deep-bosomed, broad-hipped Mary Taylor from Edinburgh at a Portsmouth ball, married her and practised in Glasgow, where he 'took a profligate advantage of his professional opportunities to make improper attempts upon his lady patients, both married and single'.

He had five children. Their nursemaid was Mary McLeod, fifteen, brown-haired, full-lipped, taut-breasted and tight-waisted below her black bombazine. She compared sexually to the wife as peach against pumpkin. Dr Pritchard slept with her while his wife was at the seaside. When Mary McLeod became pregnant in the spring of 1864, it was convenient having the doctor to abort her.

That summer Mrs Pritchard developed vomiting attacks, treated with mustard plasters and champagne. Dr Pritchard was meanwhile buying tincture of aconite by the ounce and putting it in the tapioca. Aconite is an alkaloid from monkshood root, used as a soothing ointment, poisonous to swallow in tiny doses. The doctor's mother-in-law arrived to nurse her daughter, but the following February died in the night. It was handy having Dr Pritchard to sign the death certificate, giving the cause as 'apoplexy'.

Three weeks later, his wife died in the night. He ascribed it on her death certificate to typhoid fever. The coffin was opened in Edinburgh, *en route* for burial beside mother, so that the doctor could passionately kiss the corpse's lips. He had mentioned to Mary McLeod that in the event of finding himself a widower, he would marry her. He took the train back to Glasgow and was arrested.

Some busybody had sent the Procurator-fiscal an anonymous letter. They dug up Mrs Taylor and sliced open Mrs Pritchard. Both were full of aconite (mother-in-law got it in the cheese). Everybody in Glasgow Gaol agreed what a charming fellow the doctor was. He was placidly confident of acquittal, his severest vexation lack of pomatum for his beard. He was such an agreeable man that he confessed after conviction to both murders, removing nagging doubts from jurymen's minds. He could suggest no reason for his behaviour except 'being somewhat excited by whisky'.

Pritchard was one of the last men – certainly the last doctor – to be publicly hanged in Scotland (he attracted an audience of 100,000 on Glasgow Green). The last doctor to be publicly hanged in England was William Palmer, another delightful fellow. He was thirty-one, handsome, softly bearded and whiskered, a jolly sportsman, an ideal husband, his mother-in-law's idol. He had, like myself, the advantage of education at St Bartholomew's Hospital. 'Idle, dissolute, vulgar and stupid. He scarcely practised and was chiefly engaged on the turf,' assessed Bart's Warden Sir James Paget, the Queen's Sergeant-Surgeon and the only medical man to earn mention in Gilbert and Sullivan.

Dr Palmer became a general practitioner at Rugeley in the English Midlands. He was a regular churchgoer and reliable subscriber to the

Missionary Association. He murdered his young racing friend John Cook – who had just collected a £2000 win – in the local inn on 21 November 1855. Ten minutes later, the chambermaid found him going through the corpse's pockets. Like Dr Cream, Dr Palmer used strychnine, the showy poison. As the town's doctor, he demanded an invitation to the postmortem. They noticed him trying to steal the jar containing the stomach. He later offered the post-boy a tenner to smash it on its way to the London train. He sent the local coroner a barrel of oysters and a brace of pheasants. He had earlier paid for John Cook's coffin and funeral, for speedier interment. He had done all he could.

He was arrested amid such local hatred that they had to try him in London at the Old Bailey. The defence tried to pass off his victim's violent fits, writhing agony and screams as symptoms of tetanus, a disease which could happen to anybody. 'But when the jury returned into court,' observed the sporty doctor, 'and I saw the cocked-up nose of the perky little foreman, I knew it was a gooser with me.'

It turned out that he had already murdered his wife and brother and eleven friends, for the insurance. They returned him to the Midlands for ceremonial retribution. He was hanged outside Stafford Gaol at eight o'clock on Saturday 14 June 1856. It was a depressingly wet morning (for Dr Pritchard the showers had held off, it was a lovely day), everyone with umbrellas, the doctor having to pick his way through the puddles, concerned over the mud on his boots. At St Bartholomew's we are still sensitive about our fellow-doctor's end, and explain he was attending an open-air meeting in an important capacity when the platform unfortunately collapsed beneath his feet.

Sir Thomas Overbury, poet and essayist was murdered in the Tower of London in 1613 with an arsenic and mercury enema administered by apothecaries Richard Weston and James Franklyn. They were hit-men for the young Countess of Somerset, who objected to Sir Thomas calling her 'that filthy base woman'. The penalty for poisoning was boiling alive, but the two apothecaries got off with a hanging. The Earl and Countess of Somerset were condemned to death as well, but being noble got off completely.

Dr Levi Weil from Leyden was hanged at Tyburn in December 1771 for a fatal mugging in the King's Road, Chelsea (a watch and £65).

American Dr George Lamson brought a delicious currant-studded, almond-topped Dundee cake for his wife's young brother at Blenheim House boarding school in Wimbledon. The lad died that night. Dr Lamson had chosen aconite, the easily detectable poison which dished Dr Pritchard. Traces of it were found in the boy's tuck-box. The doctor stood to inherit £2000, and was having trouble over cheques on an invisible bank-account. 'The doctor is a specially dangerous man when poor,' warned Bernard Shaw. Dr Lamson was hanged in April 1882 at Wandsworth Gaol, just north of the Wimbledon tennis.

Equally dangerous young Dr Edmé Castang poisoned his patients Hippolyte and Auguste Ballet with the newfangled drug morphine in Paris in 1823. He forged wills leaving him 100,000 francs down and 10,000 a year. The primrose path to the guillotine.

Dr Smethurst got away with it. Only just.

He was condemned to death at the Old Bailey on 19 August 1859 for poisoning his wife Belle. (*Another* Belle? Isobels should never marry doctors.) She was his second and bigamous one. He was fifty-four (he said forty eight), small, with a red moustache. Belle was forty-two, his wife seventy-four. Belle was a bilious sort.

After two months' vomiting and diarrhoea, Dr Smethurst was arrested for giving her arsenic. He was released on bail, she died the next day, he was re-arrested for murder. They found no arsenic, only traces of antimony. The professor who had earlier discovered arsenic in her stools apologized in court that the arsenic came from impurities on the copper gauze used for testing.

Antimony could have contaminated Belle's stomach medicines, like Napoleon's. Their general practitioner, Dr Julius, whose suspicions had started everything, held his doctorate from the Archbishop of Canterbury, under a statute of Henry VIII. Belle was six weeks pregnant, the vomiting time. When the post-mortem details made a juryman faint, the judge declared it was 'quite unnecessary to go into these matters with such minuteness'.

Uproar after the verdict. Leaders in the *Lancet* and *BMJ*, letters to *The Times*, petitions to the Home Secretary. They sent everything to Sir Benjamin Brodie, the richest surgeon in London. He recommended a free pardon. 'All professions are conspiracies against the laity,' said Bernard Shaw, too.

Mean-minded chemists suggested that the day between arrests Dr Smethurst dosed his wife with potassium chlorate, which invalidates the tests for arsenic. It was described in a *Lancet* of 1844, containing Dr Smethurst's own paper *On the Excision of Teeth*. He got a year for bigamy, but won an action against Belle's family over the will. He went for the hat-trick with a petition for official compensation but lost.

Dr Smith of St Fergus in Aberdeenshire shot farmhand William McDonald in 1853 and left him in a ditch (£2000 suicide-inclusive life insurance). He got away with 'Not Proven' at Edinburgh in ten minutes.

Dr Warder killed his three wives with aconite in Brighton, but escaped hanging in 1866 with cyanide at the Bedford Hotel, opposite the West Pier.

When a doctor goes wrong he is the first of criminals, pronounced Sherlock Holmes; he has the knowledge and the nerve. Perhaps that was an elementary mistake. Uneducated thugs like Dillinger and Capone would sneer at these amateurish killers, inviting arrest with the generosity of martyrs, as neurotically unbalanced afterwards as Macbeth. Perhaps the everyday dealer in life and death takes too casually the serious business of killing somebody. Perhaps he feels another one or two one way or another will never be noticed. Perhaps the bunglers were the only ones found out, and wilier doctors are getting away with murder every day.

Only one doctor has been accused of murder at the Old Bailey since World War II. He was acquitted. Perhaps we are just becoming a more respectable profession.

19 Can We Drink Our Own Health?

The Greeks did it. Lovely actress Sarah Miles does it. Maurice Wilson, the Englishman who tried to climb Mount Everest on his own, did it. Indian politicians do it, without giving a thought. Their people bathing in the Ganges do it. Other people bathing in swimming-pools *possibly* do it.

In 1695 they were doing it for 'Epilepsies, Vertigoes, Apoplexies, Convulsions, Lythargies, Migraine, Palsie, Lameness, Numbness.' Between the wars, Mr J W Armstrong did it to cure cancer, nephritis, leukaemia, heart failure, malaria, swollen testicles, bedwetting, syphilis, pierced eyeballs, the common cold and a mysterious case. It is all in his book *The Water of Life*, reprinted five times in the last dozen years.

A Yorkshireman did it to cure his cancer, and also used it as aftershave. A French dentist made a fortune from it as mouthwash. You can lose two stone a fortnight on it, if you rub it in as well. Russian peasants sold it to Paris, for inclusion in hormonal soaps and face-creams.

The elixir is free, conveniently available, and stored at body temperature. Its taste, fresh in the early morning, is 'merely somewhat bitter and salty' – I am prepared to take Mr Armstrong's word for it – 'not nearly as objectionable as, say, Epsom salts'.

The first sip is assuredly more daunting than the first dry martini. But you soon get used to either, knocking them back with smiles of increasing amiability. Perhaps you can develop addiction to it, getting yourself arrested in peculiar places when driven to satisfy your tragic craving.

It is ninety-six per cent water. It has a specific gravity between 1001 and 1025. It is usually acid. It is about one per cent ordinary salt.

It has some fifty known constituents, from adrenalin to uroporphyrin, including iron, lead, magnesium, mercury, oestrogens and 4-Hydroxy-3-methoxymandelate. It enjoys the present fad for 'alternative medicine' (gracious living quackery) through containing the breakdown chemicals of our hormones. These are formed in the liver and excreted by the kidneys. Restoring them to a body which has them circulating anyway is taking clinker to Newcastle.

If the habit spread, it could devastate the wine and spirit trade.

'No thank you, *sommelier*, we don't need the wine list, just four glasses and where are the toilets?'

The jokes are as nauseating as the practice.

20 Is the Loch Ness
Monster Human?

The Loch Ness mystery is solved.

It is as straightforward as a diagnosis of measles.

Study the case history.

The most intensely observed streak of water in the world lies five miles from Inverness, a city as grey as a plate of porridge. Loch Ness is a mile wide, twenty-four long, running south west to fill the top half of the Great Glen – *Glen More nan Albin* in Gaelic – the 300-million-year-old geological fault which slices Scotland in two. On the steep northern shore stand Drumnadrochit village and Castle Urquhart, names which alone suggest terrible stirrings in the deep. The low irregular castle ruins (created by the English in 1692) run darkly against the water, as menacingly as the smile from a broken-toothed witch.

The Loch's twenty-two square miles are fifty-two feet above sea level, its depth 700 feet, its bottom flat, its water fed by eight rivers and forty burns, abundant in oxygen and turbid with peat. Its cramped shape produces an abrupt temperature gradient, the warm surface as immiscible with the water below as a film of oil, and often banked into peculiar patterns by the wind. The *Geographical Magazine* of 1908 reported mirages of steamers, towering cliffs, snow-capped mountains, all floating in the air, from warming of the cool night atmosphere in early morning. Oddly, this is the best time of the day to see the Monster.

The Scots say nothing floats in Loch Ness. Not even Mrs Hambro of the London banking family, drowned after a motor-boat explosion in 1932 and never seen again. 'Loch Ness well deserves to be diligently studied,' said Dr Johnson in 1773.

Until 1933 the only way from Inverness at the top of Loch Ness to Fort Augustus at the bottom was a track along the southern bank, cut by English General Wade to keep the Scots in their places 200 years earlier. The afternoon drive of Mr and Mrs Mackay along the newly opened northern road just after Easter on Friday 28 April was enlivened by a 'tremendous upheaval' in the flat, calm loch.

'The creature disported itself, rolling and plunging for fully a minute, its body resembling that of a whale, and the water cascading and churning like a simmering cauldron,' the *Inverness Courier* reported on 2 May. 'Apart from its enormous size, the beast, in taking the final plunge, sent out waves that were big enough to have been caused by a passing steamer.'

Oddly, nobody else noticed the afternoon's spectacular.

The *Courier* wore a serious face, named the apparition 'the Monster', emphasized that Mr Mackay was a respected businessman, Mrs Mackay a university graduate.

More oddly, the *Courier* omitted that Mr and Mrs Mackay ran the Drumnadrochit Hotel.

The conjurers of the press turned the Monster from a big fish in the little pool of local journalism to a huge one in the Fleet Street horsepond.

Lord Beaverbrook's *Daily Express* interviewed horrified hikers, alarmed anglers and fainting females before whom the Monster had reared into view, though oddly the commotion in mid-loch was never glimpsed by more than one knot of people at a time. Lord Rothermere's *Daily Mail* was famous for stunts – three years before, it paid toothy London typist Amy Johnson £10,000 to fly solo to Australia in twenty days. The *Mail* mounted an expedition. It hired an African big-game expert, dispatched him as the Trader Horn of the Flying Scotsman. Its reward was a headline in September 1933, MONSTER OF LOCH NESS IS NOT A LEGEND BUT A FACT. The white hunter found its footprints on the shore.

While plaster of Paris casts were rushed to the London Zoo, the tracker reconstructed his quarry as a powerful animal twenty feet long which could breathe through a nostril poked unobtrusively above water.

He was right.

The footprint was a hippo's, made by a larky Scotsman's umbrella stand. Its pursuer had overlooked the Monster's walking on one leg.

Then the Monster was photographed. The (unabashed) *Daily Mail* published the picture on 21 April 1934, taken by a Harley Street gynaecologist, Robert Kenneth Wilson, a highly respectable professional man. He was up there photographing wildfowl. The picture has no shoreline and bears an odd resemblance to a bird wallowing on the ripples. It has entered Loch Ness hagiology as 'The Surgeon's Photograph', though oddly it was taken on 1 April, All Fools' Day.

The local hotels were crammed even at Christmas, when Inverness has the touristic magnetism of Baffin Island. The council went mad and floodlit the town. Bertram Mills' circus offered £20,000 (now the best part of half a million) to have the Monster gambolling on its sawdust. It became a music-hall joke. When the dragon entered during *Siegfried* at Covent Garden, the audience giggled.

Like most cults, it sadly suffered schism. True believers affirmed that the new road exposed the Monster to the world. Heretics protested that it only exposed more simpletons to the water. Superstition roots like heather on the mist-drenched Highland soil. Every loch had its black man-eating water horse, the *each uisge*, the kelpie. Travellers tempted to mount were galloped adhesively into the loch and their livers washed ashore the next morning. The kelpie could become a randy youth (identifiable by the hooves). Resourceful Sarah MacFinlay, propositioned by one, saved her honour by tantalizing it until the water boiled in her clay groggan and dashing it over his amorous parts.

The Monster was reported fifty-two times in 1933, thirty-nine times in 1934, then only nineteen more times over the five years until World War II. Devotees emphasize that the voyeurs were such soberly reliable persons as lawyers, municipal dignitaries, a whole abbeyful of Bendictine monks at Fort Augustus and Harold Macmillan's sister-in-law. During the war, a Royal Navy motor-launch captain ascribed his dented bow to ramming the Monster, but the Admiralty was not amused.

The postwar Monster made literary reputations. A dozen books appeared about it. What someone has troubled to write in a book is true to another who has taken the trouble to read it. What appears on television is *ipso facto* true to everyone – a chilling half-hour on brain death on *Panorama* brought a confetti of torn-up kidney donor cards.

In the summer of 1960, an aeronautical engineer showed on TV fifty feet of film depicting something a mile away moving erratically towards the opposite shore, where it sank. It had reminded him through binoculars of an African buffalo. Buffalo or dead cow, Nessie was sighted only twenty-eight times during the previous fifteen years, but after appearing on television was seen ten times before Christmas. Seek, and ye shall find.

Water bailiff Alex Campbell appeared on TV forty times to recount his seventeen meetings with the Monster, one only twenty-five yards away when it rose gently one calm day between boat and shore. Oddly, Mr Campbell was the local correspondent of the *Inverness Courier* who had reported the seminal sighting by the Mackays.

The most successful Monster-watcher was a Cockney greengrocer encamped on the bank, who observed it for six seconds on twenty-seven occasions, a total exposure of two minutes and forty-two seconds, infinitesimal compared with himself on television.

A Loch Ness Investigation Bureau was founded in the spring of 1962 by Sir Peter Scott, naturalist son of Scott of the Antarctic. It used searchlights to attract Monsters like moths. Fifty volunteers manned ten observation posts from first light to last, clutching forms asking themselves forty questions. The Bureau inaugurated a committee of inquiry – two naturalists, a marine biologist and a lawyer – who that winter decided 'there is some unidentified animate object in Loch Ness,' on the photographic evidence of two long shapes, one vertical shape and three domes. After ten years the Bureau closed down, despite an injection of £1000 from the Highlands and Islands Development Board – a canny investment in the goldmine down the glen.

Science belatedly caught Nessie by the tail. A Texan went down in a yellow submarine. The RAF spied the loch for a month by autogyro. Birmingham University plumbed it with sonar. In 1970, Dr Robert Rines of the Boston Academy of Applied Science arrived like Batman.

Dr Rines was not a scientist but a patent lawyer, who ran the Academy with his brother-in-law in his spare time. He deployed sidescan sonar, stroboscopic lights, electronic cameras and powerful hormonal baits. Four of his underwater films sent to the California Institute of Technology in Pasadena for computer enhancement showed the flipper of a large animal. Or of a very small animal. The Smithsonian Institution in Washington thought it was the tail of a newt. The Natural History Museum in London said dryly, 'Information in the photographs is insufficient to enable identification.'

Dr Rines was back next summer with $250,000 worth of equipment. It was on the afternoon of 19 June 1975 that he found the Monster. He took six underwater photographs of it in colour. It had flippers, a long neck and a horned head, just like the ones on the Inverness anti-litter posters, comic postcards and shortbread tins, the cross between a cobra and Donald Duck, but better nourished.

The world was to greet the Monster in December at a joint meeting of the Edinburgh Royal Society and Edinburgh University, suggested by Sir Peter Scott. He made paintings of the flippered humped beasts swimming underwater with forgivably smug grins. He christened them scientifically *Nessiteras rhombopteryx* – oddly, the anagram of 'Monster hoax by Sir Peter S.' Bookmakers shortened the odds against from 100–1 to 6–1.

The Natural History Museum said, 'The photographs do not constitute acceptable evidence of the existence of a living animal…a whole variety of speculative interpretations seems equally plausible.' Spoilsports. They thought it a bit of tree. Other people thought it a bit of weed, peat particles, a farmer's plastic sack, a fragment of the life-size model monster made during filming *The Private Life of Sherlock Holmes*, a disintegrating bap (Highland doughnut).

Edinburgh University drew a sharp breath. They suspected showbiz rather than science. The symposium was cancelled. The unveiling was transferred to a room in the House of Commons, where fancies stalk the corridors unnoticed.

To Nessie's friends the photographs were a plesiosaurus, a fish-eating reptile extinct for 70 million years. They recalled with justified glee that the equally extinct coelacanth was fished alive from the Indian Ocean in

1938. Certainly, this reduced the 10,000 known extinct animals by one, but was achieved in the coelacanth's known environment. What was a tropical, ocean-going plesiosaurus doing in Loch Ness?

What does it eat? Harvard calculated from the Loch's food stocks that a fifty-foot Monster must weigh the same as a six-foot sturgeon.

How does it breathe? It must at least *once* a year – record submersion for a hibernating turtle in the laboratory.

It must defaecate, but no excreta has been washed ashore.

It must reproduce, but no eggs have surfaced.

It must die, but where are the bodies? Dead men and monsters must float in time from decomposing gases, like weather balloons.

Are its bones interred like men's? Nessie swallows stones for post-mortem ballast, say the believers. So do crocodiles, but dead crocs float. Ah, but not in Loch Ness. Nothing floats. Newton was hit by the apple under his chin.

'Unless one is prepared to brand more than 3000 people whose names and addresses are available as either fools or liars, it is hard to see how any unbiased person can disregard this weight of evidence,' wrote the Loch Ness Investigation Bureau about the Monster-sighters.

They were neither. They were normal human beings.

Mankind mercifully has an infinite capacity for self-deception. Even the scientific evaluation of new drugs demands an elaborate 'double-blind' technique, neither patient nor doctors knowing who takes potion or placebo.

Oddly, seeing is not believing. It is only seeing what we believe we see. Which is often what we expect to see. Or what we are encouraged to see, particularly if everybody else believes they saw it too.

Our vision is more elaborate than our Polaroids. The retina converts light through the eye's lens into impulses transmitted by the optic nerves, which partially cross over at the base of the brain. We see by our optic cortex, in the back of our heads. More complicated still, the inner parts of both retinas register on the opposite side of the brain, from the outer parts on the same side. So brain injury can cause partial blindness in each eye.

The brain affects our sight like a computer intervening between camera lens and film. The sensation from the eye selects an hypothesis from the mind to fit the object seen, like a busy barmaid selecting the right drink from half-heard orders in a crowded pub. This is useful for inferring the characteristics of things we observe only bits of. We know our desk has four legs, though we see only the two front ones, because we know that otherwise it would fall over backwards.

Likely objects are thus created by the brain – even the most sober and intelligent brains – regardless of their real existence. Three black circles, each with a slice removed like a cake, easily hold a non-existent triangle. The concave mould of a human face is seen as a normal convex one, the notion of a hollow face being too outlandish for our powers of perception. Objects appear different to us in different contexts. The identical outline of a man's hand can change its anatomy to a girl's hair or a horse's tail, a shoe can be an axe, a leg its handle. What we expect to see, we do.

Watchers who expect to see monsters on Loch Ness will continue seeing them in every ripple, shadow, log, dead dog, swimming stag or rising trout. We will continue seeing UFOs in seagulls or in Venus. We see pictures in the fire, as the Canadians saw the Devil in the Queen's hair on a dollar bill, and the Argentines Evita's bottom on a ten-peso one. We see ghosts in flapping curtains and moonlight's shadows, as we once saw witches riding broomsticks through the scudding clouds and our future in tea-leaves.

Heed a moment a neuropsychologist.

'The experimentally elusive, but nevertheless vital feature of perception, is that it *goes beyond the available sensory evidence*… Illusions are important as *phenomena of perception*…these can be specific phenomena of perception which, though generated by brains, are not part of the physical world of objects.'

Man suffers as universally from deficient eyesight as from susceptibility to hoaxes. Expeditions and volunteers have a reasonable urge to justify themselves. The earnest discussion of monsters makes them no more real in the scientific age than in the Middle Ages,

In 1982, a biological expedition scanned Loch Ness with sonar day and night for more than 1500 hours from May to August. On two mornings and two afternoons they found traces which were 'far more powerful than would come from kinds of fish, were recorded at great depth and are apparently moving quickly…This may be the monster, or it may not.'

This does not seem much from fifty years' frenzied observation and investigation. Look at a map of the world. The possibility of an extinct animal inhabiting an insignificant Scottish creek, against human beings seeing things which are not there, as they do every day, is infinitesimal.

But long live Nessie, even if you cavort only in the mind! You afford delightful holidays in glorious scenery. What would the local B and B season do without you? ('B and B' means 'bed and breakfast', a sign that hangs from Scottish homes as did once the targe and claymore.) You provide a healthy summer's occupation for students. You kindle the warmth of companionship in a common cause. You are more fun than CND. Best of all, you provide the excitement of scientific research and the stimulus of scientific controversy, without the tedium of scientific discipline or the bother of acquiring a scientific education.

21 Will More Amazing Medical Breakthroughs Let Us Live for Ever?

This dramatic improvement [in mortality over the past one hundred years] has led many people to inquire whether mankind might, under ideal conditions, live for much longer periods. In fact, however, (to oversimplify) we seem to have an inbuilt biological clock that ensures that only very few will survive for more than one hundred years.

Professor Sir Richard Doll, *Harveian Oration*, 1982

22 Is Jesus a Good Doctor?

OLD MEDICAL JOKE.

Examiner: Now, my boy, you're deep inside the abdomen performing a splenectomy. The spleen comes off in your hand. What do you do?

Student: Er – apply a clip to the splenic artery.

Examiner: You can't. The artery's retracted like a nervous snail in a thunderstorm.

Student: Er –

Examiner: Come on! The abdomen's filling up with blood like a kitchen sink.

Student: Ah! I'd suck the blood out, sir.

Examiner: The theatre sucker's on the blink. Well? The blood's now slopping on the floor.

Student: I should pray, sir.

Examiner: Oh? Wouldn't you send for a consultant surgeon before calling on the assistance of an unqualified practitioner?

Jesus had a mixed and busy practice in His short spell among us. He treated leprosy (there was a lot of it about at that time of the millennium), fever, the 'lame, blind, dumb, maimed', epilepsy, a manic-depressive at Capernaum and a schizophrenic Gadarene (it went into the swine).

Also a woman with a twelve-year history of uterine bleeding who 'had suffered many things of many physicians, and had spent all that she had, and was nothing bettered, but grew rather worse' – a sadly persistent predicament – another woman bowed for eighteen years by tubercular

Pott's disease of the spine, a case of heart failure with oedema, and the restoration of an embarrassingly severed ear (the high priest's servant's). 'Rise, take up thy bed, and walk' was pronounced to a man paralyzed for thirty-eight years. He lay among 'a great multitude of impotent folk' at the pool of Bethesda, by the Jerusalem sheep-market. You can still see it in St Bartholomew's Hospital, on the staircase of the Great Hall, the only mural Hogarth executed.

Jesus' most successful case occurred at Bethany, between Jerusalem and the Dead Sea. He had already resuscitated children on the point of death ('the damsel is not dead, but sleepeth'), but Lazarus was assuredly dead for four days, because 'he stinketh'.

The corpse was buried in a cave blocked by a stone. Jesus cried with a loud voice, 'Lazarus, come forth!' He walked out, 'Bound hand and foot with graveclothes: and his face was bound about with a napkin.' It must have given everyone quite a turn.

'And His fame went throughout all Syria,' reported Matthew. 'And they brought unto Him all sick people that were taken with divers diseases and torments, and those which were possessed with devils, and those which were lunatick, and those that had the palsy, and he healed them.'

For reasons of His own, Jesus did not as miraculously abolish all sickness and all sin, creating mass redundancy in the medical and clerical professions.

Achieving miracles is easy.

Nineteen-and-a-half centuries later, a family doctor had a pitiful patient afflicted with progressive deafness. He had endured it with the fatalism of advancing age, seeking no medical advice until someone got through to him that the provision of free hearing-aids for its senior citizens was written into the British Constitution.

The doctor saw through his speculum hard, brown, glistening wax, tight as the corks in a couple of bottles of vintage port. The smelly, sticky mess was extracted in fragments by vigorous application of syringe and warm water.

'You can go home now,' the doctor said amiably. 'No need for hearing-aids.'

The patient stared in wonder. He breathed, '*I can hear!*' He jumped up. '*I can hear!*' he cried. 'I can hear! I can hear!' he exclaimed, running round the packed waiting-room. 'It's a miracle!' he shouted, bursting into the street, grabbing shoppers. 'I can hear!'

The doctor was amused at such touching faith. Next morning the patient was back, with the deaf, halt, dumb, blind and palsied of the neighbourhood for a repeat divine performance.

Jesus is now risen to consultant. His main surgery is Lourdes.

Lourdes is a town of 20,000 people, 12,000 feet up the Pyrenees halfway between Biarritz and Andorra. It has sickness as Las Vegas has gambling.

In the first half of 1858, fourteen-year-old Bernadette Soubirous, daughter of an out-of-work miller, had eighteen visions in a cave in the cliffs bordering the fast-flowing Gave de Pau. Response was mixed, pubescent girls often seeing things (as Loch Ness Monster, see Chapter 20). The parish priest backed her, local curiosity warmed with the season to excitement, which blazed into awe on the sunny morning of 2 March. On her way home from the cave, Bernadette stripped the bandages from a sick girl's eyes *who could see!* (Indeed she could, bright light irritated her eyes, she wore bandages as sunglasses.)

On 25 March, Bernadette saw the Virgin Mary. The cave echoed with gasps of wonderment. The police had to erect crowd-barriers. The mob stormed them flat. The police put them back. Anyone seeing visions was threatened with arrest.

Tout-Paris now talked of Lourdes. In July, the infant Prince Imperial caught sunstroke at Biarritz. His life was saved at Lourdes, so that it could be lost twenty years later by British incompetence in Zululand.

Jesus' success was ensured by a fellow-Jew, Monsieur Archille Fould, who brought the railway there in 1866. Lourdes was opened to Europe, like the *Côte d'Azur*. Pilgrims were sped from the United States in 1874, from heretical England in 1883. In 1950 the airport opened (ex-Luftwaffe). Lourdes now received 5,000,000 visitors a year. In the Michelin it boasts three times the hotels of Monte Carlo, if its restaurants have only the chilling spoon and fork.

Travel agents rejoice at a saintly patience towards cost-cutting which would raise riots on the Costa del Sol ('Hotel overbooked? Arrange an all-night vigil'). Hotel staff are the only gnashers of teeth, pilgrims being poor tippers. The property values match Paris.

The *Cité Religieuse* fills the elbow of the river. It has two basilicas, overground and underground (in case of rain), the miraculous baths, and the cave, now the Grotto. The steep streets across the bridge are lined by shops crammed with the tawdry props of piety – Virgin Marys in plaster and plastic, with batteries for glowing or flashing, with detachable heads to fill with holy water, piles of rosaries, medals, postcards (they send 2,000,000 of them in July and August). Bernadette became a nun in Nevers ten years after her visions, died ten years later of tuberculosis, aged thirty-five. You can see her in a glass coffin in the Nevers Convent of St Gildard. She has been dug up three times.

The bedridden arriving at Lourdes are manhandled by strapping *brancardiers* – stretcher-bearers – into the wards of the Seven Sorrows Hospital. They are later as efficiently arrayed in stretchers and chairs on the *Esplanade des Processions*, as though awaiting medical attention instead of priests and nuns playing doctors and nurses.

Everyone is praying, even the busy *brancardiers*. 'Prayers have the value of ritual,' explained a cleric in the Sunday papers, 'praying for the sick is on a level with taking them flowers.' Our eternally underprivileged invalids can delight in a transient usefulness, through their cherished prayers for the healthy.

Every afternoon comes the Blessed Sacrament Procession, each pilgrimage with its banners, its climax the blessing of the sick. The Procession raises the hope which Émile Zola perceived in his novel *Lourdes* (banned in Lourdes), 'that nothing was beyond the power of Heaven, and that if it were Heaven's pleasure they themselves would all become healthy, young and superb.' It is only a faint hope, because the claimed cures are so rare. Were the hope stronger, the cruelty would lie unbearably on the conscience.

The second moment of hope flickers like St Elmo's fire in the baths. No matter it is Lourdes tap-water – the medicinal waters of Vichy, Bath or Baden-Baden have no effect taken externally. The thirteen baths open at seven in the morning for six hours, immersing 6500 pilgrims a day, eighty per bath per hour, a dip of three-quarters of a minute each, share the water. 'Persons suffering from the syphilis, cancer, tuberculosis, and all manner of diseases are immersed in the same bath water,' reveals *The Mystery of Lourdes*. 'Strangely, no infection seems to result.' We must be thankful for small miracles.

The doctor sees no more mysticism in disease than in the mites of Stilton cheese. This exaggeration and exploitation of emotion in sickness, the ceremonial applied to the clinical, the dramatization of the cure, the slight to science, the creation of moral capital from human suffering, vary to most medical people from the gigglesome to the gruesome.

'To cure sometimes, to relieve often, to comfort always' are the doctor's aims, expressed by Dr Edward Livingstone Trudeau of the Adirondacks. Most diseases beyond dietary deficiencies, bacterial assault and anatomical faults are incurable. They are mostly relievable, often to negligibility. Others sadly leave sufferers feeling like Zola's of 1891.

Condemned, abandoned by science, weary of consulting doctors, of having tried the torturing effects of futile remedies. And how well one could understand that, burning with a desire to preserve their lives, unable to resign themselves to the injustice and indifference of Nature, they should dream of a super-human power, of an almighty Divinity who, in their favour, would perchance annul the established laws, alter the course of the planets, and reconsider His creation!

They turn to fashionable 'alternative medicine' – though alas, There Is No Alternative. They turn to the ageless quack. They turn to Lourdes.

St Augustine defined a miracle as an occurrence contrary to what is known of Nature.

There are three reasons for medical ones.

1. The symptoms are psychological and removed by psychological influences.
2. Many diseases remit and relapse – get better or worse.
3. The doctor has made the wrong diagnosis.

Lourdes has worked sixty-four miracles since 1858. Those performed before World War II are too remote in medical history to justify study. (Jesus' miracles are infinitely so). Of eighteen from 1945 to 1978, four would fit into Category 1 and ten into Category 2. This leaves a case of Addison's disease – adrenal gland failure – one of bony cancer in the pelvis, one cancer of the uterine cervix (followed-up for only two years), and a case of Hodgkin's disease, fatal in 1950, but from the case history perhaps innocuous glandular fever.

The doctors of Lourdes, like doctors elsewhere, did not suspect the treacherous deceptions and self-deceptions in assessing new cures. Clinical trials with placebos have become so self-critical that neither doctor nor patient now knows who is firing the live rounds or blanks.

Nor would a doctor who cured the incurable, with anything from interferon to aspirin, risk his reputation and his profession's by proclaiming it without a substantial series of successes. The cures of Lourdes may be miracles, but they are statistically insignificant ones. Those who claim the benefit of supernatural healing cannot credibly claim also supernatural rules. St Augustine would assuredly have agreed.

We World War II medical students were taught by retired consultants substituting for doctors in the Forces. They brought us the medicine of the 1930s, sometimes of the 1920s. Then the doctor, like Jesus, had little to apply to the patient but his personality.

'Always leave hope,' they told us. To 'Is it cancer, doctor?' answer 'Well, it *could* be.' To 'How much longer have I? answer 'It could be years, you know.' The patient fiercely grasps the flimsy straw, hoping 'to hope till Hope creates/From its own wreck the thing it contemplates.'

Zola concluded, 'But Lourdes grew up in spite of all opposition, just as the Christian religion did, because suffering humanity in its despair must cling to something, must have some hope: and on the other hand, because humanity thirsts after illusions. In a word, it is the story of the foundation of all religions.'

We should not take Lourdes too seriously. It offers the superb comfort of hope. The good doctor Jesus knows *that* is His function, and better than his acolytes that the technicalities of medicine are best left to His technicians.

Even if no one gets cured, the weather in the Pyrenees is lovely, the companionship of the journey exhilarating, the organization businesslike, the stage-management breathtaking, and To be a pilgrim is less aimless than to be a tourist.

23 What Are Other People's Sex Lives Like?

Studies by social researchers... have shown that promiscuity is characteristic of extroverted, gregarious men and women who often give sex less importance than do the shy and introverted. Indeed an individual's attitude to sex usually seems to mirror his or her character. Selfishness, cruelty, egocentricity, and confidence or lack of it will all be reflected in sexual just as much as in social relationships. This seems to me the main lesson that adults can try to pass on to the children: that individuals vary as much in their sexual needs and capacities as they do in every other way. Moreover, children who have been brought up to respect the feelings and anxieties of others will carry the same attitude into their sexual relationships.

Dr Tony Smith, *The Times*, 14 September 1978

24 What is the Word of Freud?

I

'Our Ford – or our Freud, as, for some inscrutable reason he chose to call himself whenever he spoke of psychological matters… ' Thus Aldous Huxley foresaw in 1932 how we inhabitants of the Brave New World would create a religion of cars and sex.

'I have no knowledge of having any craving in my early childhood to help suffering humanity,' Freud wrote in Vienna during his fifties.

In my youth I felt an overpowering need to understand something of the riddles of the world in which we live and perhaps even to contribute something to their solution. The most hopeful means of achieving this end seemed to be to enrol myself in the medical faculty.

When he graduated from it in 1881, the fashionable riddles lay in the brain.

It reposed like a vast walnut in its shell of skull, trailing tapes and threads of nerves which translated thought into action. How?

So logical an enigma fascinated the French. Guillaume Duchenne, son of a Boulogne sea-captain, prowled the Paris hospitals with his electrical machine, stimulating nerves through the skin, discovering that the muscles responded in groups, tracing the paralysis of polio to the spinal cord, finding death before fame in 1875. Jean-Martin Charcot, with the squint and the rich fat wife, bestowed prestige with a seat at his lectures in

La Salpêtrière on the Left Bank, became immortalized in the flail Charcot joints of syphilis.

It fascinated Freud. He had a mechanical mind. His reputation rests on shadows, conceived and manipulated with the precision of Hitchcock shooting and cutting a tantalizing movie.

In 1885 Sigmund Freud was a lecturer in neuropathology at the Vienna General Hospital. He was discharged from military service, in which his twenty-fourth birthday was spent under close arrest for going AWOL. (Another mind which moulded the twentieth century was similarly cooled, student Karl Marx seeing the cells in Bonn for persistent drunkenness.)

Freud's imagination moved from the triggering of nerve impulses to faults of the firing mechanism. He found a wonder drug for worry – cocaine! It filled him with energy and joy. He sent it to his fiancée, petite twenty-four-year-old Martha Bernays in Berlin, 'to make her strong and give her cheeks a red colour'.

He discovered that a drop instantly anaesthetized skin, lip, tongue, eye. Chatting to doctors in the hospital courtyard, joined by another with a sore eye, Freud led the party to his room, applied cocaine, effected the cure. One of the young men was Carl Koller, burning to be an eye surgeon. He slunk off, used cocaine, dazzled Vienna with impossible ophthalmic operations, seized the invention for himself.

'This is the only way to make important discoveries, to have one's ideas exclusively focused on one central interest,' Freud drew a rueful and lasting lesson. Had Koller not been hanging about the courtyard, Freud would be remembered as a great anaesthetist.

That winter in Paris, medical magnifico Charcot vouch-safed pupil Freud the translation of his lectures into German. (He was later outraged to discover it printed with Freud's own footnotes.) After marrying Martha in 1886, Freud named his eldest son Jean Martin after Charcot. The second was Oliver, after Cromwell.

At La Salpêtrière was displayed Mademoiselle Deneuve, aged twenty-two, paralysed down the right side. It had struck the previous summer, postponing her marriage. She was bizarrely unemotional to the affliction, *la belle indifférence*. Charcot hypnotized her and cured her. The cause? *Le voilà*, the man she did not wish to marry! Freud stared with a wild surmise, upon a peak in clinical Darien.

Three years earlier in Vienna, Dr Josef Breuer (immortalized in a breathing reflex), Freud's mentor who sent him patients and lent him money, had a worse case of hysteria. 'Anna O' was sometimes totally paralysed, numb, contorted, her speech and vision distorted. Others, she was an attractive, clever young woman. Dr Breuer found accidentally that talking about each symptom removed it. He discussed them as systematically as clearing constipation with doses of castor oil. Anna was cured, and fell wildly in love with him. 'Something that is never absent,' observed Freud impassively, 'the patient's transference on to her physician.'

Freud and Breuer jointly described this mental purgation in *Studies on Hysteria* of 1893. Psychoanalysis was in business.

The early Freudians enjoyed the complacent fervour of prophets. They applied medicine to the philosophies of Schopenhauer and Nietzsche. 'Speculation, some of it endowed with the insight of genius, was allowed to run riot,' an English textbook comments severely, 'No single theoretical step was empirically confirmed before being made the basis for a further elaboration of theory.' Freud offered it whole, take it or leave it. 'Such *rigid orthodoxy* is not compatible with the spirit of science,' adds the textbook in the same spirit.

Freud attracted antagonism like a skinhead in the Athenaeum. He described hysteria in men, when everyone knew it was an exclusively female complaint. Why, it was Greek for 'womb', you could treat it with cliteroidectomy. Into the new century, a professor in Hamburg dismissed Freud's notions on sexuality: 'This is not a topic for discussion at a scientific meeting: it is a matter for the police.'

If the Viennese doctors jibbed at taking the evangelists seriously, they took themselves with sufficient seriousness for six continents. They formed the Psychological Wednesday Society, meeting weekly in the waiting-room of the famous flat at 19 Berggasse, which was over a butcher's shop. They expounded and argued over black coffee, Freud disliking 'the faint mental obfuscation that even a slight drink induces'. Instead, he played taroc.

In 1908 they became the Vienna Psychoanalytic Society, in 1910 the International Psychoanalytic Association, by 1913 they secreted a cabal to perpetuate the pure doctrine. 'I was so uneasy about what the human rabble would make of it when I was no longer alive,' Freud explained. He gave these half-dozen zealots gold rings with a Greek design, as he wore himself. Freud classified a ring as an object of rich symbolic meaning indicative of an erotic tie, but none of them needed consult a psychiatrist because they were all busy analysing each other.

For a Freudian to be analysed by Freud himself was the equivalent of an invitation to sit on the right hand of God and dip your bread in his gravy. Forty-year-old Dr Victor Tausk, handsome, blue-eyed, clipped-moustached, out of the Austro-Hungarian Army in 1919 (unpopular for a sympathetic study of deserters' psychology), impoverished, struggling to keep a family, a chronic depressive, desperate to become a psychoanalyist, implored Freud to analyse him as a start.

Tausk had been seduced before the war by Lou Andreas-Salomé, a fine-looking woman who could wear fox furs like an empress sables. She had arrived in Vienna aged fifty-two in 1912 to conquer both psychoanalysis and Freud. She had previously been having it off with Rilke and Nietzsche. Freud sent her flowers, walked her home in the small hours, found himself directing lectures at her or staring entranced at her vacant chair (when she may have been in bed with Tausk), admired her 'curiously enough without a trace of sexual attraction'. He shouldered his jealousy because Lou was his spy on Tausk, who he secretly feared would steal his ideas. He had been prickly about this since the great cocaine robbery.

Still suspicious, Freud now sent Tausk to thirty-five-year-old Helene Deutsch, who Freud was analysing himself. (She left her handbag on the couch, to Freud clearly a sexual proposition, though he dozed during their sessions, she noticed his cigar burning the carpet.) The reluctant Judas was insulted, but accepted Helene – secretly so that 'he could lie on her couch six days a week, knowing that she would be on Freud's couch just as often.' It was a discreditable *mensonge à trois*.

The triangle twisted. Helene proclaimed Tausk a genius. Freud told Helene that she must choose between them (psychoanalytically). Tausk lost. He compensated with betrothal to a patient sixteen years younger than himself, a pianist. His intellectual feminist wife had divorced him in 1908 over a dancer.

Freud was outraged. An analyst marrying a patient was comparable to a priest copulating with a nun in the confessional. Tausk was defiant. He would get a marriage licence on the Thursday morning of 3 July 1919, but during the early hours he instead drank a bottle of slivovitz and killed himself by blowing out his brains with his service revolver and strangling himself as he dropped with the rope round his neck. Freud confessed to Lou Andreas-Salomé that he did not miss him.

When forty-year-old Herbert Silberer disagreed in the Psychoanalytic Association with Freud's interpretation of dreams, Freud sent the two-line letter, 'I no longer desire personal contact with you.' On 12 January 1923 Silberer hanged himself, with a torch shining in his contorted face to greet his wife coming home from a party. These psychiatrists had their little ways. That year Sam Goldwyn offered Freud $100,000 as technical adviser on *Famous Love Stories of History* (from Antony and Cleopatra onwards). Freud wired he would not even see Goldwyn. This caused a bigger sensation in New York than King Kong.

Abrasive sects kindle self-combustion. Carl Jung stumped home to Switzerland, by 1934 was writing about 'the formidable phenomenon of National Socialism, on which the whole world gazed with astonished eyes'. Freud accused him of anti-Semitism. Not at all, protested Jung, he simply differentiated between Jewish and Aryan psychology. (Jung later won the honour of Nazi hate.)

In February 1911 Alfred Adler, who used to light Freud's cigars, denied the importance of the libido. Freud was aghast. He decided the man was a paranoiac. On 28 February Adler deserted to found the Society for Free Psychoanalysis. The psychiatrists, their wives and friends took sides, intellectual dinner-parties in Vienna became impossible.

Hungarian Sandor Ferenczi invented in 1931 the 'kissing technique'. He thought his patients needed motherly affection. Freud thought it would lead to pawing, peeping, showing and you-know-what. When they met, Freud refused his hand, turned his back, stalked from the room. He thought Ferenczi was a paranoiac, too.

The man who shins the intellectual Matterhorn needs rope himself to yes-men. Ernest Jones from Cardiff, fiery as a scuttle of Welsh nuts, was analyzed by Ferenczi in 1913, wrote the Freud biography, did a night in a London cell accused of indecency towards small children. Hans Sachs mimicked Freud to his cigars and panic at missing trains, in the 1920s was organizing summer holidays for psychiatrists and their patients in a caravan (the Monty Python team could do something with this).

Freud's cases were the cult's miracles. Little Hans never left home through terror that the horses would bite him, but this was really because horses had big penises, bigger even than his father's, which was naturally bigger than Little Hans', which he unconsciously wished to put up mother.

The Rat Man was concerned at the possibility of undergoing a Chinese torture with a pail of rats secured to the behind, to tunnel their escape with their teeth through the anus. It arose from once feeling his governess' genitalia. The Wolf Man dreamed the tree outside his bedroom window was crammed with wolves like the starlings, after observing aged eight his parents' copulation. A failure was Miss Lucy, an English governess haunted by the smell of burnt pudding.

The Hapsburg monarchy was a terminal case, but Vienna was a prosperous capital, baroque and rococo to the lifestyle of its amiable inhabitants. Below them ran like the Third Man's sewers a shifty, shiftless population from an empire of squabbling Slavs bossed by Germans. Sadly Freud never netted one of the polyglot drifters in 1910. Fellow-inmates at the men's hostel at 27 Meldermannstrasse might have clubbed for the 1000-kronen fee, exasperated by his noisy and excitable behaviour.

He was twenty-one, always in need of a shave and haircut, in greasy bowler and long black overcoat presented by a Hungarian-Jewish old clothes man. He made cheap paintings of the Schönbrunn Palace and St Stephen's Cathedral for furniture shops. He spent his day in the public library, obsessed by social movements and politics. He had this paranoia about the Hapsburgs, Slavs, Catholics, Social Democrats and particularly Jews (with apologies to Herr Professor, who would surely understand).

A successful consultation might have spared the world much painful worked-out fantasy.

II

God used 744,746 words in the Bible. Freud wrote three million to propagate his own doctrines.

Freud's Ideas

1 THE UNCONSCIOUS
Freud invented the cuckoo-clock mind. The cuckoo chirps out, unaware it is driven by a slowly unwinding hidden spring. If the spring goes wrong, so does the cuckoo.

2 THE OEDIPUS COMPLEX
Every little boy wants to kill father and marry mother. He worries that father wishes to castrate him over this.

The situation need not disturb everyday family life.

The Oedipus Complex describes unconscious motives. It is not to be taken more literally than the mother who tells her naughty child I'll skin you alive, or the worker who tells his foreman to go and stuff his capstan lathe. It is curbed by the instinctive barrier against incest ('rolling your own'). Even fantasizing about incest makes man feel terribly guilty. Hamlet was a sad case.

The counterpart of the Oedipus Complex completes a Sophocles double-bill with the Electra Complex (in some rural areas not so damn theoretical).

3 THE LIBIDO
'According to the prevailing view, human sexual life consists essentially in an endeavour to bring one's own genitals into contact with those of the opposite sex,' wrote Freud. No argument.

Sex for Freud starts not at puberty but at birth. Sucking is sensual for babies. So is doing poo-poos. He differentiated 'genital'– the straightforward

121

juxtaposition – from 'sexual' which colours every scene of life. The libido is the psychological energy driving both, like the electricity which powers tools and keeps existence comfortable.

Freud's teaching did for copulation what television did for evenings.

'In those pre-Freudian days,' Nancy Mitford wrote about Madame de Pompadour, 'the act of love was not yet regarded with an almost mystical awe; it had but a limited importance. Like eating, drinking, fighting, hunting and praying it was part of a man's life, but not the very most important part of all.'

4 THE EGO AND THE ID

The sophisticated ego interprets the world to the uncouth, instinctive id. The super ego restrains the id from contaminating the ego.

'These psychoanalytical theories suggest that man is essentially a battlefield, he is a dark cellar in which a maiden aunt and a sex-crazed monkey are locked in mortal combat, the affair being refereed by a rather nervous bank-clerk,' comments another psychiatrist.

5 THE INTERPRETATION OF DREAMS

Man has been fascinated by dreams as long as by the stars.

However absurd, shameful or confused, dreams represent the fulfilment of unsatisfied desires the day before. These escape past the super ego but *in disguise*, like Cinderellas past a dozing Ugly Sister to a masked ball. Dreamer Prince Charming dances the night away without recognizing them. It had already happened in Vienna, to Herr von Eisenstein with his masked housemaid Adele and masked wife Rosalinde at Prince Orlofsky's ball in *Die Fledermaus*.

The dancers brandish the lost property of the mind. Dream about an umbrella, it is a penis. So are trees, daggers, rifles, watering-cans, pens and pencils, hammers, fountains, snakes and fish, your hat and coat. Bottles and buckets, suitcases and pockets, cupboards and cookers, rooms, ships, churches, anything hollow are the female genitalia, also doors, tables, books, snails and mussels.

'The remarkable characteristic of the male organ which enables it to rise up in defiance of the laws of gravity' had Freud's patients dreaming happily of Zeppelins. 'Dreams of flying, so familiar and often so delightful, have to be interpreted as dreams of sexual excitement,' smiled Freud, anticipating the Mile High Club by a century.

Those horrifying anxiety dreams – falling off cliffs, naked in the supermarket – depict more compellingly seductive desires romping round you all night.

Freud put it all in *The Interpretation of Dreams*, which appeared in 1899 and in six years sold 351 copies.

It has its critics.

'As Jocasta said to Oedipus,' recalled Professor Eysenck, ' "Many young men dream of sleeping with their mothers"; if they do, why should they at times go to the trouble of dreaming that they are shooting off a revolver at a cow?'

Said Gowing to Mr Pooter, 'There is nothing so completely uninteresting as other people's dreams.'

6 PENIS ENVY
Little girls like playing with dolls because they represent penises. This is because a doll makes a little girl a mother, and mother has a penis like daddy. Later this assumption is found to be incorrect. It makes girls difficult in their teens.

7 FREUDIAN SLIPS
The treacherous disclosure of repressed desires. Favourite medical student example – salesman displaying car to delicious girl, 'This model is the cuntessence of quimfort.'

Includes unconscious detours to avoid irksome acquaintances, leaving things where you long to return, losing things because you have rowed with donors. Four days running, Freud forgot to drop into the stationer's to buy more blotting-paper – *Fliesspapier*. He was quarrelling tormentedly with his homosexual friend in Berlin, nose-surgeon Dr Wilhelm Fliess.

8 THE PLEASURE PRINCIPLE
'The ego strives after pleasure and seeks to avoid unpleasure.' Good idea.

Pleasure from relief of tension is heightened by delay, whether opening the bowels, having an orgasm, reading a detective novel or like Freud incubating ideas for years before publication. This is *Beyond the Pleasure Principle*.

9 THANATOS

The death instinct. We all have it. The impatient commit suicide. The rest of us take it easy, with drink and drugs, smoking and speeding, gluttony and sloth.

10 HYSTERIA

Symptoms without physical cause, developed for real or imagined advantage from motives largely unperceived by the patient. The Wooden Horse for honourable escape from our difficulties.

The malingerer shams symptoms, the hysteric endures them. 'Hysterics suffer mainly from reminiscences,' said Freud. Cure is effected by their expulsion in an outpouring of the painful emotions they once provoked.

Canst thou not minister to a mind diseas'd,
Pluck from the memory a rooted sorrow,
Raze out the written troubles of the brain...

Macbeth was demanding of the resident psychiatrist at Glamis three centuries before Freud thought of it.

11 PSYCHOANALYSIS

Curing illness with words. You transfer emotional pains to the mind of your psychiatrist. Your resistance to this induces hostility towards him (or her). Your success induces your falling in love with him (or her).

The dictionary defines, '*Freudian* (coll) indirectly or subconsciously sexual.' Freud's sex life was as dreary as Robinson Crusoe's.

He loathed contraception (condoms constructed with the stoutness of tyres for Herr Daimler's automobiles). He played pelvic Russian roulette with coitus interruptus, and Martha was annoyingly fertile. At thirty-five she declared she had reached the menopause, but it was Anna.

Freud sighed, 'If we could succeed in raising the responsible act of procreating children to the level of a deliberate and intentional activity and in freeing it from its entanglement with the necessary satisfaction of a natural need… '

He shuddered, 'The harm that is inherent in sexuality in general, sexuality being one of the most dangerous activities of the human being… '

He bewailed, 'Virtue accompanied by full potency is usually felt as a hard task… '

Freud's sister-in-law Minna, fatter but four years younger than Martha, warmer and wittier, lived in the flat over the butcher's from the age of thirty-one, 'Tante Minna' in her little lace cap. She said to Jung in 1907 that she was having a raving affair with Freud, or Jung said she said. She partnered Freud on holidays because Martha suffered from *Reisflieber* (Freud's diagnosis). The only way into Minna's bedroom was through the Freuds'. How terrible to wake bursting for a pee, the sole route through the room with the world's greatest psychiatrist in bed with your sister his wife.

A biographer discerns, 'Freud's horror and fear of the female genitalia can be read into his account of his dream life.'

Freud's only physical reaction to homosexual Fleiss was fainting fits (he fainted also at the sight of blood). Freud referred to their meetings as a 'congress', but this was only a Freudian slip.

He gave up sex with Martha at forty-one. Five years later he discovered at a house party 'a young girl who was staying there as a guest and who aroused a feeling of pleasure in me which I had long thought was extinct.' I wonder who she was.

The busy cobbler's children go barefoot, the erudite psychiatrist's are reared like the kids next door. When his sons asked where babies come from, Freud sent them to the family doctor to find out. He warned young Oliver against masturbation (not adding it would make him blind). He was angry at another son for having sex with a young lady under analysis (the lad could hardly be surprised at father getting to hear). He ticked off his daughter-in-law for eternally cuddling her baby. He dismissed his wife's migraine as merely physical. He was less fussy than the American psychiatrist who took a spanner to his daughter's bicycle lest the seat were too stimulating – anticipating the early Betjeman,

I often think that I should like
To be a saddle on a bike.

Freud always tended to wet his pants. At sixty-seven a lifetime of cigar-smoking claimed its pound of flesh and he developed cancer of the palate. Otto Rank broke into hysterical laughter. Freud's speech grew impaired, he wore a false roof to his mouth, he suffered thirty-one operations – including Professor Eugen Steinach's, a vasectomy performed to atrophy the reproductive tissue of the testis and stimulate the hormonal, bringing rejuvenation. It always failed, though it did wonders for old rats. Freud had it to vanquish the death instinct by stimulating the life instinct, a curious stroke of psychosurgery.

The crass and brutal Nazis invaded Austria in 1937, proscribed Freud's works as Jewish pornography, arrested his daughter Anna. His escape was achieved by American ambassador to Paris William C Bullitt, whose urgings stirred President Roosevelt little. A ransom was paid by a princess descended from Napoleon's brother. The Nazis forced attestation that he had been treated 'with all the respect and consideration due to my scientific reputation, that I could live and work in full freedom, that I could continue to pursue my activities in every way I desired... ' Freud added to his signature, 'I can heartily recommend the Gestapo to anyone.'

The Nazis issued an *Unbedenklichkeitserklärung*, he left on 4 June 1938, settled in Hampstead in north London, read Agatha Christie and died on 23 September 1939.

We take pride that the bones of Darwin and Newton lie among us. We may take as much that Freud and Marx chose to lay them here. 'I was one of those who have "disturbed the sleep of the world", as Hebbel says,' claimed Freud. He may have delineated only a blueprint of fairyland, but he was right.

The phlegmatic British took slowly to Freud. He was cherished by the Bloomsbury Set (Virginia Woolf was schizophrenic). The Psychoanalytic

Society excitedly printed 100,000 translations of a Freud book and sold 500. The cynical French did not take to him at all. In America — which Freud described as 'a mistake; a gigantic mistake, it is true, but none the less a mistake' — he became one of its major industries.

Otto Rank had borne the doctrine when Freud fell ill in 1923, and became rich ('the rat leaving the sinking ship,' said Freud). Helene Deutsch enjoyed a film-star arrival in 1930, in the New York papers a ravishing tall German blonde, though she was short, dark and Polish. 'The psychoanalytic approach fits in extremely well with dominant *American biases*,' explains the same severe English textbook.

It is of a mechanistic and deterministic type which suits well a society based on the exploitation of the machine...in the relative significance it gives to *mother and to father*, it fits American upbringing as well as, or even better than, the home life of the child in an Austrian-Jewish family, which was its starting point.

America grew after Faraday, the civilization of the scientific age. There is always a man to fix (for a fee) your car, your TV, your wrinkles, your public image. Why not your mind?

Psychologists' wrangles over Freud resemble the theological arguments to which true believers prefer to be indifferent and casual worshippers ignorant. Freud is the god of our comfortable, complacent, carnal society, neither wrathful nor loving, but consolingly imperturbable, who in his infinite mercy renders our most disgraceful behaviour as guiltless as catching a cold.

If he had not existed, it would be necessary to invent him.

25 O Death, Where is Thy Sting?

In our graveyards with winter winds blowing
There's a great deal of to-ing and fro-ing
But can it be said
That the buried are dead
When their nails and their hair are still growing?

British Medical Journal, 13 November 1982

26 Why Do So Many Doctors Write Books?

'I do not know a better training for a writer than to spend some years in the medical profession,' wrote Somerset Maugham, who qualified in 1897 from St Thomas' Hospital opposite the Houses of Parliament.

He also mentioned, 'Writing is so pleasant a profession that it is not surprising if a vast number of persons adopt it who have no qualifications for it.'

In the summer of 1882, twenty-three-year-old Dr Conan Doyle (MB Edinburgh) set up a brass plate at Bush Villa, Southsea, the genteel end of Portsmouth. He had to polish it himself (after dark), sweep the floors, sleep on a mattress of the straw packing his medicine bottles, his pillow Bristowe's *Principles of Medicine* wrapped in his other suit.

Worse still, he had to open his own front door. He perfected the air of happening to be in the hall while the parlourmaid was below stairs. Only caller of the week was a top-hatted man who suffered from bronchitis, but had come to collect on the gas-meter.

Luckily, Dr Doyle's grocer was an epileptic. They struck a bartering arrangement. When the patient had fits the doctor had butter. Then the wretched fellow died, reducing him to dry bread and saveloys.

'The throb of the charwoman's heart and the rustle of the greengrocer's lungs' never made Dr Doyle more than £300 a year. He gambled on becoming an eye specialist, took two months in Vienna (the lectures were unfortunately incomprehensible through ignorance of medical German), rented rooms in Harley Street — 'A waiting-room and a consulting-room, where I waited in the consulting-room and no one waited in the waiting-room.' So he wrote about Sherlock Holmes from ten to four instead.

The character better know than Hamlet or Don Quixote was created by a medical education.

'Spot diagnosis' was the clinical craze. A girl working on the lucifers – making matches – was gleefully identified by phosphorous burns on her fingers. A sweatshop sempstress' left index finger was recognizably roughened from needlepricks, a coachman's finger and thumb by the reins. Wee, sharp-faced, forty-three-year-old Dr Joseph Bell of Edinburgh could tell a copyist by the corn on his middle finger from a violinist with them on the tips of all four.

Out-patients at the Edinburgh Royal Infirmary fascinated surgical dresser Doyle.

'Well, my man, you've served in the army?' Dr Bell addressed the next patient.

'Aye, sir,' replied the civilian, mystified.

Dr Bell instantly declared him a recently discharged non-commissioned officer of a Highland regiment stationed in Barbados.

'You see, gentlemen,' he explained to the students with insufferable cleverness, 'the man was a respectful man but did not remove his hat. They do not in the army, but he would have learned civilian ways had he been long discharged. He had an air of authority and he is obviously Scottish. As to Barbados, his complaint is elephantiasis, which is West Indian and not British.'

Elementary, my dear Hippocrates.

Conan Doyle was so impressed that he depicted Sherlock Holmes as Dr Bell, 'with a great hawk's-bill of a nose, and two small eyes, set together on either side of it'. Everyman's Sherlock Holmes, lantern-jawed, beetle-browed, with insanitary pipe and lethally conspicuous headgear, is the younger brother of artist Sydney Paget, model for his illustrations in the *Strand Magazine* of 1891. (James Robertson Justice is now as much Sir Lancelot Spratt to me as to his delighted audiences.)

'The precise and intelligent recognition and appreciation of minor differences is the real essential factor in all successful medical diagnosis' – Dr Joseph Bell's words are enduring. 'Eyes and ears which can see and hear,

memory to record at once and to recall at pleasure the impressions of the
senses, and an imagination capable of weaving a theory or piecing together
a broken chain or unravelling a tangled clue, such are the implements of
his trade to a successful diagnostician.'
You know my methods, Watson!
Dr Watson was another educated at St Bartholomew's Hospital. In the
Bart's pathology department you can see the chair he sat on when first
meeting Holmes –

> 'Dr Watson, Mr Sherlock Holmes,' said Stamford, introducing
> us.
> 'How are you?' he said cordially, gripping my hand with a
> strength for which I should hardly have given him credit. 'You have
> been in Afghanistan, I perceive.'
> 'How on earth did you know that?' I asked in astonishment.

And we're off.

Dr Doyle became Sir Conan in 1902 for writing *The Cause and Conduct of
the War in South Africa*, proving that Great Britain was jolly well in the right
all along. In the end he floated into spiritualism, giving lectures with
photographs of fairies.

Medicine, that subdivision of the humanities, decided Thomas Mann.
Church and Law were the ancient professions on which the intellect
flowered. Medicine was a stunted growth, but had its blossoms.

Sir Thomas Browne (MD Leyden 1633, MD Oxford 1637), practitioner
in Norwich, was erudite, mystical and sceptical – equally about his
profession ('I that have examined the parts of a man and know upon what
tender filaments that Fabrick hangs, do wonder that we are not always
sick.') as about himself ('We are but embryon philosophers... A dialogue
between two infants in the womb concerning the state of this world might
handsomely illustrate our ignorance of the next.'). He was learnedly
edited by Maynard Keynes' surgical brother (another Bart's man).

Oliver Goldsmith (MB Oxford 1769), in practice at Southwark, south of
the Thames, developed the clinical technique of examining patients while

holding his hat – to hide the patches on his coat, occasioned by 'his irreclaimable habits of dissipation', as Thackeray put it. Through reviewing Viennese Dr Leopold Auenbrugger's *Inventum Novum Percussione Thoracis Humani* in 1761, Oliver Goldsmith made a sensational breakthrough in English medicine – he introduced percussion of the chest.

Tobias Smollett (MD Aberdeen 1750) practised in Bath until his paper *On the External use of Water* proved the Bath waters were exactly like the water anywhere else. Autocrat of the breakfast table Oliver Wendell Holmes (Professor of Anatomy, Harvard, 1847–82) christened anaesthesia. Henry VIII's doctor Andrew Boorde (Oxford and Montpellier) was 400 years ahead of his time with *The Dyetary of Health*. Rabelais (MD Montpellier 1537) had like most doctors a Rabelaisian sense of humour.

Frederich von Schiller, surgeon to the Würtemberg regiment in 1781, did better professionally than Johann Wolfgang Goethe, who failed to qualify at Strasbourg, a setback suffered also by Eric (*Juan in America*) Linklater, C S (Hornblower) Forester, Francis (*The Hound of Heaven*) Thompson, Christopher (*I Am a Camera*) Isherwood and Sydney (witty) Smith.

In the profession's poets' corner reposes John Keats (LSA Guy's 1861), dead at twenty-five in Rome from tuberculosis, Abraham Cowley (MD Oxford 1657), George Crabbe (doctor and curate at Aldeburgh, Suffolk) and Robert Bridges (our only Poet Laureate from St Bartholomew's so far).

Dr Samuel Smiles (MD Edinburgh 1833, aged twenty) never required help. Dr Mark Roget (MD Edinburgh 1798, aged nineteen) was never at a loss for a word. Sir Frederick Treves (FRCS 1878, London Hospital), master mariner, appendicectomist to Edward VII, had to wait sixty years until his *Elephant Man* hit Broadway. To Dr Anton Pavlovich Chekhov (MD Moscow 1884) medicine was his wife, the stage was his noisy, flashy, insolent mistress, who luckily kept him.

Dr Warwick Deeping (Cambridge) in the 1920s, Dr A J Cronin (Glasgow) in the 1930s, Dr Frank Slaughter (Johns Hopkins) in the 1940s made doctors as famous for the readability of their writing as the illegibility of their script. We scrawl because we must write much, fast and often standing up. Medicine is the crowded, rushed, everlasting, skilled handling of people who are sick – and of those who are well and helping you, who are often the more difficult. It is an occupation as different from an author's as anchorman from anchorite.

Somerset Maugham wrote,

> I saw the gallantry that made a man greet the prognosis of death with an ironic joke because he was too proud to let those about him see the terror of his soul.

And,

> I have more than once seen men die, peacefully or tragically, and never have I seen in their last moments anything to suggest that their spirit was everlasting. They die as a dog dies.

And,

> The Professor of Gynaecology. He began his course of lectures as follows: 'Gentlemen, woman is an animal that micturates once a day, defaecates once a week, menstruates once a month, parturates once a year and copulates whenever she has the opportunity.'
> I thought this a prettily-balanced sentence.

He could not have so written had he not been a doctor. But the literary man gains more from the medical one than a stock-in-trade of life and death. The writer without a sense of values is a colour-blind painter.

Birth, and copulation, and death,
That's all the facts when you come to brass tacks said Eliot.

The good doctor who handles such fundamental items every day teaches himself to distinguish the really important from the really *un*-important in human affairs and human relationships. The good novelist instinctively senses it.

John Brown (MD Edinburgh 1833) wrote in *Rab and His Friends*,

Don't think medical students heartless; they are neither better nor worse than you or I: they get over their professional horrors, and into their proper work; and in them pity as an *emotion*, ending in itself or at best in tears and a long drawn breath, lessens, while pity, as a *motive*, is quickened, and gains power and purpose. It is well for poor human nature that it is so.

That explains why many of us took up medicine. The privilege of educated compassion for the infinite, fascinating fancies and frailties of human beings explains why some of us write books as well.

Acknowledgements

With gratitude, to the Wellcome Institute for the History of Medicine, the library of the Royal College of Surgeons of England, the library of St Bartholomew's Hospital Medical College and the London Library.

References

1   **Why Did Mary Toft Give Birth to Seventeen Rabbits?**

Seligman, S A, Mary Toft – the rabbit breeder. *Medical History*, 1961, 5: 349–60.

Thompson, C J S, *Mysteries of history*. London: Faber & Gwyer, 1928: 185–93.

Mitford, N, *The sun king*. London: Hamish Hamilton, 1966.

Ault, N and Butt J (eds), *The poems of Alexander Pope* (4th edn). London: Methuen, 1954: 259–62.

2   **Whose Teeth Did George Washington Eat With?**

Woodforde, J, *The strange story of false teeth* London: Routledge & Kegan Paul, 1968: 98–108.

3   **Was the Marquis de Sade Really a Kindly Man?**

Hayman, R, *De Sade*. London: Constable, 1978.

Thomas, D, *The Marquis de Sade*. London: Weidenfeld & Nicolson, 1977.

Sade, Le Marquis D-A-F de, *The 120 days of Sodom and other writings*. New York: Grove Press, 1968.

Beauvoir, S de, Faut-il brûler Sade? *Les temps modernes*. Dec. 1951 and Jan. 1952.

Price, J H, *A synopsis of psychiatry*. Bristol: Wright, 1982.

Mitford, N, *Madame de Pompadour*. London: Sphere. 1970.

Deleuze, G, *Sacher-Masoch*. London: Faber. 1971.

5   **What Put Carlyle Off His Food?**

Haliday, J L, *Mr Carlyle my patient*. London: Heinemann. 1949.

Bett, W R, *The infirmities of genius*. London: Johnson, 1952: 11–22.

Froude, J A, *My relations with Carlyle*. London: Longmans, Green, 1903.

Wilson, D A, *The truth about Carlyle*. London: Alston Rivers, 1913, 60–9.

Harris, F, *My life and loves*. New York: Grove Press, 1963: 232–4.

Sutherland, J (ed.), *The Oxford book of literary anecdotes*. Oxford: Clarendon, 1975.

Crichton-Browne, Sir J Froude and Carlyle, *British Medical Journal*, 1903, **i**, 1498–502.

7 Dr Barnardo a Medical Waif?

Wagner, G, *Barnardo*. London: Weidenfeld & Nicolson, 1979.

Walbrook, H M, *Murders and murder trials 1812–1912*. London: Constable, 1932: 281–307.

British Medical Journal, 1888, **ii**, 769.

Bell, D, *The Province*, 12, 19 and 26 August 1979.

9 Was Napoleon Killed by His Wallpaper?

The new Cambridge modern history (vol. 9). Cambridge: Cambridge University Press, 1969.

Lachouque, H, *The last days of Napoleon's empire*. London: Allen & Unwin, 1966.

Martineau, G, *Napoleon's St Helena*. London: Murray, 1968.

Chaplin, A, *A St Helena's who's who*. London: self-published, 1914.

Weider, B and Hapgood, D, *The murder of Napoleon*. London: Robson, 1982.

Forshufvud, S, *Who killed Napoleon?* London: Hutchinson, 1962.

Richardson, R G, How sick was Napoleon? *History of Medicine*, 1981, **225**: 109–11.

Jones, D, The singular case of Napoleon's wallpaper. *New Scientist,* 1982, **96**: 101–4.

New Scientist, 1982, **96**: 257.

The Times, 23 October 1982.

Leslie, A C D and Smith, H, Napoleon Bonaparte's exposure to arsenic during 1816. *Archives of Toxicology,* 1978, **41**: 163–7.

Parry, L A, *Some famous medical trials.* London: Churchill, 1927: 96–7.

Anderson, J R, *Muir's textbook of pathology* (11th edn). London: Arnold. 1980.

Taylor, A J P, *Europe: grandeur and decline.* Harmondsworth: Pelican, 1967: 71

11 Did Hitler Need Glasses?

Heston. L L and R, *The medical casebook of Adolf Hitler.* London: Kimber, 1979.

Bezimensky, L, *The death of Adolf Hitler.* London: Michael Joseph, 1968.

Stierlin. H, *Adolf Hitler: a family perspective.* New York: Psychohistory Press, 1976: 11

Shiver, W L, *The rise and fall of the Third Reich.* London: Secker & Warburg, 1960.

Taylor, A J P, *English history 1914–1945.* Oxford: Clarendon, 1965: 176.

Observer Magazine, 22 September 1968.

Daily Telegraph, 22 December 1982.

12 How on Earth Do You Do Female Circumcision?

Bettelheim, B, *Symbolic Wounds.* London: Thames & Hudson, 1955: 252–60.

World Medicine, 14 January 1976: 44–7.

World Medicine, 22 January 1983: 24–5.

British Medical Journal, 1979, **i**: 1163–4.

Oliver, J E, *British Medical Journal,* 1979, **ii**: 933.

Kenyatta, J, *Facing Mount Kenya.* London: Secker & Warburg, 1938.

14 Is Cannibalism Fattening?

Read, P P, *Alive!* London: Secker & Warburg, 1974.

Tannahill, R, *Flesh and blood*. London: Hamish Hamilton, 1971

Hogg, G, *Cannibalism and human sacrifice*. London: Hale, 1958.

Frazer, Sir J G, *The golden bough* (abridged edn). London: Macmillan, 1950: 497–9.

Mayer-Goss, W, Slater, E and Roth, Sir M, *Clinical psychiatry*. London: Cassell, 1955: 302.

Deuteronomy 12:16.

16 Is Smoking Good for Us?

Doll, Sir R, Prospects for prevention. *British Medical Journal*, 1983, **i**: 445–53.

The Times, 3 February 1983.

World Medicine, 28 July 1979.

18 Do Doctors Make Good Murderers?

Smith, Sir S, *Mostly murder*. London: Harrap, 1959: 227–36.

Parry, L A, *Some famous medical trials*. London: Churchill, 1927.

Walbrook, H M, *Murders and murder trials 1812–1912*. London: Constable, 1932.

Blundell, R H and Haswell Wilson, G (eds), *Trial of Buck Ruxton*. London: Hodge, 1937.

Parry, L A (ed.), *Trial of Dr Smethurst*. Edinburgh: Hodge, 1931.

Roughead, W (ed.), *Trial of Dr Pritchard*. London: Sweet & Maxwell, 1906.

Lancet, 29 October 1910: 1299–1301.

Medvei, V C and Thornton, J L, *The Royal Hospital of Saint Bartholomew 1123–1973*. London: St Bartholomew's Hospital, 1973: 72.

Gilbert, W S, *Patience*, 1881, Act I.

Monro, T K, *The physician as man of letters, science and action* (2nd edn). Edinburgh: Livingstone, 1951: 186–96.

19 Can We Drink Our Own Health?

Armstrong, J W, *The water of life* (2nd edn). Saffron Walden: Health Science Press, 1971.

The Times, 24 March 1983.

20 Is the Loch Ness Monster Human?

Whyte, C E, *More than a legend*. London: Hamish Hamilton, 1975.

Dinsdale, T, *Loch Ness monster*. London: Routledge & Kegan Paul, 1961.

Witchell, N, *The Loch Ness story*. Lavenham: Dalton, 1976.

Mackal, R P, *The monsters of Loch Ness*. London: Macdonald & Jane's. 1976.

Searle, F. *Nessie*, London: Coronet, 1976.

Gregory, R L, *Visual perception*. Oxford: Oxford University Press, 1973.

Shine A, The biology of Loch Ness. *New Scientist*, 17 February 1983. 462–7.

Daily Mail, 25 March 1983.

22 Is Jesus a Good Doctor?

Fuller, R H, *Interpreting the miracles*. London: SCM Press, 1963.

Zola, E, *Lourdes* (trans. E A Vizetelly). London: Chatto & Windus, 1929.

Cranston, R, *The mystery of Lourdes*. London: Evans, 1956.

Marnham, P, *Lourdes*. London: Heinemann, 1980.

Sunday Times, 28 September 1980.

24 What Is the Word of Freud?

Jones, E, *The life and work of Sigmund Freud*. London: Hogarth, 1953–57.

Roazen, P, *Freud and his followers*. London: Allen Lane, 1976.

Roazen, P, *Brother animal*. London: Allen Lane, 1970.

Stafford-Clark, D, *What Freud really said*. London: Macdonald, 1965.

Wollheim, R, *Freud*. London: Fontana, 1971.

Foss, B M (ed.), *New horizons in psychology*. Harmondsworth: Penguin, 1966.

Eysenck, H J, *Sense and nonsense in psychology*. Harmondsworth: Penguin, 1957.

Mayer-Goss, W, Slater, E and Roth, Sir M, *Clinical psychiatry*. London: Cassell, 1955.

Lindford Rees, W L, *A short textbook of psychiatry*. London: English Universities Press, 1967.

Shirer, W L, *The rise and fall of the Third Reich*. London: Secker & Warburg, 1960.

26 Why Do So Many Doctors Write Books?

Pearson, H, *Conan Doyle*. London: Hamish Hamilton, 1943.

Conan Doyle, Sir A, *Sherlock Holmes: the complete long stories*. London: Murray, 1929: 10.

Monro, T K, *The physician as man of letters, science and action* (2nd edn). Edinburgh: Livingstone. 1951.

Maugham, W S, *The summing up*. London: Heinemann, 1938.

Maugham, W S, *A writer's notebook*. London: Heinemann, 1949.

RICHARD GORDON

DOCTOR IN THE HOUSE

Richard Gordon's acceptance into St Swithin's medical school came as no surprise to anyone, least of all him – after all, he had been to public school, played first XV rugby, and his father was, let's face it, 'a St Swithin's man'. Surely he was set for life. It was rather a shock then to discover that, once there, he would actually have to work, and quite hard. Fortunately for him, life proved not to be all dissection and textbooks after all… This hilarious hospital comedy is perfect reading for anyone who's ever wondered exactly what medical students get up to in their training. Just don't read it on your way to the doctor's!

'Uproarious, extremely iconoclastic' – *Evening News*
'A delightful book' – *Sunday Times*

DOCTOR AT SEA

Richard Gordon's life was moving rapidly towards middle-aged lethargy – or so he felt. Employed as an assistant in general practice – the medical equivalent of a poor curate – and having been 'persuaded' that marriage is as much an obligation for a young doctor as celibacy for a priest, he sees the rest of his life stretching before him. Losing his nerve, and desperately in need of an antidote, he instead signs on with the Fathom Steamboat Company. What follows is a hilarious tale of nautical diseases and assorted misadventures at sea. Yet he also becomes embroiled in a mystery – what is in the Captain's stomach-remedy? And, more to the point, what on earth happened to the previous doctor?

'Sheer unadulterated fun' – *Star*

RICHARD GORDON

DOCTOR AT LARGE

Dr Richard Gordon's first job after qualifying takes him to St Swithin's where he is enrolled as Junior Casualty House Surgeon. However, some rather unfortunate incidents with Mr Justice Hopwood, as well as one of his patients inexplicably coughing up nuts and bolts, mean that promotion passes him by – and goes instead to Bingham, his odious rival. After a series of disastrous interviews, Gordon cuts his losses and visits a medical employment agency. To his disappointment, all the best jobs have already been snapped up, but he could always turn to general practice…

DOCTOR GORDON'S CASEBOOK

'Well, I see no reason why anyone should expect a doctor to be on call seven days a week, twenty-four hours a day. Considering the sort of risky life your average GP leads, it's not only inhuman but simple-minded to think that a doctor could stay sober that long…'

As Dr Richard Gordon joins the ranks of such world-famous diarists as Samuel Pepys and Fanny Burney, his most intimate thoughts and confessions reveal the life of a GP to be not quite as we might expect… Hilarious, riotous and just a bit too truthful, this is Richard Gordon at his best.

RICHARD GORDON

GREAT MEDICAL DISASTERS

Man's activities have been tainted by disaster ever since the serpent first approached Eve in the garden. And the world of medicine is no exception. In this outrageous and strangely informative book, Richard Gordon explores some of history's more bizarre medical disasters. He creates a catalogue of mishaps including anthrax bombs on Gruinard Island, destroying mosquitoes in Panama, and Mary the cook who, in 1904, inadvertently spread Typhoid across New York State. As the Bible so rightly says, 'He that sinneth before his maker, let him fall into the hands of the physician.'

THE PRIVATE LIFE OF JACK THE RIPPER

In this remarkably shrewd and witty novel, Victorian London is brought to life with a compelling authority. Richard Gordon wonderfully conveys the boisterous, often lusty panorama of life for the very poor – hard, menial work; violence; prostitution; disease. *The Private Life of Jack The Ripper* is a masterly evocation of the practice of medicine in 1888 – the year of Jack the Ripper. It is also a dark and disturbing medical mystery. Why were his victims so silent? And why was there so little blood?

'...horribly entertaining...excitement and suspense buttressed with authentic period atmosphere' – *The Daily Telegraph*

882377

Printed in Great Britain by
Amazon.co.uk, Ltd.,
Marston Gate.